PRACTICAL SOCIAL WORK

Series Editor: Jo Campling

(BASW)

Social work is at an important stage in its development. All professions must be responsive to changing social and economic conditions if they are to meet the needs of those they serve. This series focuses on sound practice and the specific contribution which social workers can make to the well-being of our society in the 1980s.

The British Association of Social Workers has always been conscious of its role in setting guidelines for practice and in seeking to raise professional standards. The conception of the Practical Social Work series arose from a survey of BASW members to discover where they, the practitioners in social work, felt there was the most need for new literature. The response was overwhelming and enthusiastic, and the result is a carefully planned, coherent series of books. The emphasis is firmly on practice, set in a theoretical framework. The books will inform, stimulate and promote discussion, thus adding to the further development of skills and high professional standards. All the authors are practitioners and teachers of social work, representing a wide variety of experience.

JO CAMPLING

PRACTICAL
SOCIAL WORK
Series Editor: Jo Campling

BASW

Social Work with Disabled People

Michael Oliver

MACMILLAN

First published in 1983
Reprinted 1987, 1989

Published by
MACMILLAN EDUCATION LTD
Houndmills, Basingstoke, Hampshire RG21 2XS
and London
Companies and representatives
throughout the world

Printed in the People's Republic of China

ISBN 0-333-32707-1 (paperback)

Contents

7 **Conclusions: Some Professional and Organisational Aspects of Social Work with Disabled People** 118

Acknowledgements

The author and publishers wish to thank the following who have kindly given permission for the use of copyright material:

Bedford Square Press of the National Council for Voluntary Organisations for an extract from *Disabled People – A Right to Work?* by R. Grover and F. Gladstone.

Basil Blackwell Publishers Ltd for extracts from *Provision for the Disabled* by E. Topliss; *A Charter for the Disabled* by E. Topliss and B. Gould; *Occupational Survival* by C. Satyamurti; *Children, Grief and Social Work* by G. Lonsdale, P. Elfer and R. Ballard; an article by T. Booth in *The Practice of Special Education*; and *Theory and Practice in Social Work* by R. Bailey and P. Lee.

Central Council for Education and Training in Social Work for extracts and a table from *Social Work: People with Handicaps Need Better Trained Workers*, Paper 4 (1974).

The Controller of Her Majesty's Stationery Office for data from *Handicapped and Impaired in Great Britain* by A. Harris.

The Editor, *Health and Social Service Journal*, for an extract from an article 'Psychological effects of physical disability' by Jayne Ibbotson.

V. Finkelstein for extracts from *Disability and Professional Attitudes* (NAIDEX Convention, 1981) and *Attitudes and Disabled People* (World Rehabilitation Fund, 1980).

Heinemann Educational Books for extracts and a table from *The Meaning of Disability* by M. Blaxter.

Hodder & Stoughton Educational for extracts from *Handicap in a Social World* edited by Brechin, Liddiard and Swain, and *Children with Handicaps* edited by Selfe and Stow.

The NFER–Nelson Publishing Company Ltd for extracts from *An Ordinary Place* by R. and L. Tuckey.

The Open University Press for extracts from 'Adopting a life style' and 'Family circles' by J. Swain, and 'The individual behind the statistics' by V. Carver, from Course Unit P251 *The Handicapped Person in the Community*.

Penguin Books Ltd for extracts from *Poverty in the United Kingdom* by Peter Townsend (Allen Lane/The Penguin Press 1979) Copyright © Peter Townsend 1979.

Pergamon Press Ltd for extracts from *Spinal Cord Injuries* by R. B. Trieschmann.

Pluto Press Ltd for an extract from *The Political Economy of Health* by L. Doyal.

Martin Robertson & Co. Ltd for extracts from *Disability in Britain* by Walker and Townsend.

Rochdale Voluntary Action for an extract from *Housing and Disability: A Report on the Housing Needs of Physically Handicapped People in Rochdale* (1978).

Routledge & Kegan Paul Ltd for extracts from *Professional Power and Social Welfare* by P. Wilding; and *The Handicapped Child and His Family. The Family Fund: An Initiative in Social Policy* by J. Bradshaw.

Sage Publications Ltd. London, for extracts from *Cross National Rehabilitation Policies: A Sociological Perspective* edited by Gary Albrecht.

W. F. R. Stewart for extracts from *The Sexual Side of Handicap*.

Wayland Publishers Ltd for an extract from *Blinded in War: A Model for the Welfare of all Handicapped People* by F. le Gros Clark.

Every effort has been made to trace all the copyright holders but if any have been inadvertently overlooked the publishers will be pleased to make the necessary arrangements at the first opportunity.

Foreword

During the past three years when the ideas in this book have been germinating and the writing taking place, I have been fortunate to have the support of three different groups of people. To the Open University team responsible for the course *The Handicapped Person in the Community*, to the Development Group of Kent Social Services Department and the Social Work Staff Group at the University of Kent, I owe an immense debt of gratitude.

Three individuals have also been crucially important in the writing of this book: my wife Judith, who not only provided love and support but also made a significant intellectual contribution to the work; Frances Hasler, friend and colleague at the Spinal Injuries Association, provided pertinent comments and interest; and Ann Kittle typed and retyped the manuscript so efficiently that I was able to concentrate solely on the task of putting ideas into words.

Finally, my gratitude extends to all students on the Post-Qualifying Course in Social Work and Physical Handicap at the University of Kent who provided me with a stimulating environment in which to test and develop my ideas as well as adding a critical perspective to my wilder flights of fancy.

Readers may well ask why with such help and support the book is not better than it actually is. Any deficiencies are of course my own responsibility. I only hope that the two groups at which the book is aimed, social workers and disabled people, will feel neither misrepresented nor betrayed by it, and that it may provide a useful framework around which to organise their mutual activities.

University of Kent, 1982   Michael Oliver

List of Tables and Figures

Tables

Figures

Introduction: Setting the Scene

Much has been written in recent years about what social work is and indeed what it is not. There have been careful and systematic attempts to map out its territory, and these have been met by polemics suggesting that social work cannot do half what it claims to do; indeed its ultimate survival has been questioned. However, while recognising that there is therefore much dispute over the nature of social work, this is no place to pursue such disputes. Instead a brief description of what the term 'social work' means as used here will be outlined and this will then be related to current issues including the relationship between theory and practice, the role of social work and its relationship to disabled clients.

The term 'social work' as used here refers to organised professional activity carried out on behalf of individuals or groups of clients. This activity is geared towards the provision of services on an individual group or community basis. The adjective 'professional' implies that those who provide these services are certified as competent to do so and are financially rewarded for so doing. The provision of such services does not merely involve the matching of need with resources but will also require professionals to be involved in ascertaining what needs are and arguing for adequate resources to meet those needs. The context of such activity may be a social services department, a hospital, residential accommodation, a voluntary organisation or any other appropriate agency. The range of methods involved will include casework, group-work and community work, and these may be applied in a variety of settings including the home, residential care, day care and sheltered accommodation.

This is obviously a very broad definition of social work and flies in the face of criticisms, for example by Brewer and Lait (1980), that social work has taken on far more tasks than it is capable of effectively carrying out. Indeed, more sympathetic 'insiders' like the Association of Directors of Social Services, in their submission to the Barclay Committee, called for a more restricted role for social work, focusing largely upon the individual and the provision of counselling and casework services. The Barclay Committee (1982) developed a view of social work practice similar to the position being taken in this book, though Professor Pinker in his note of dissent took a line broadly the same as the ADSS submission. More will be said about the Barclay Report in the final chapter.

While there may be adequate and justifiable reasons for calls upon social work generally to narrow its base of activity, it is not appropriate in the field of physical handicap, for it will be argued throughout this book that disability is not an individual problem. Rather, it is a social problem concerned with the effects of hostile physical and social environments upon impaired individuals, or even a societal one concerned with the way society treats this particular minority group. As such, the base for social work activity with disabled people needs to be broadened, not narrowed. As has recently been suggested:

> Many disabilities are the result of social conditions and amenable to social services intervention. Medical care treatment, for example, is not going to solve the low-income, social isolation, and architectural barriers that are major for the disabled. At issue is the conflict over bureaucratic supremacy between the medical and social service parts of government. The clash involves ideological and theoretical differences concerning the nature of the problem and the response.
>
> (Albrecht and Levy, 1981, p. 23)

There is also the question of the relationship between theory and practice in social work. There is much disillusionment with 'ivory-tower academics' whose theorising is not based upon the realities of practice, and again, there may well be some justification for this disillusion in social work generally. The idea of social work as a practical activity is of course politically appealing. *Social Work with Mentally Handicapped People* by Christopher Hanvey (1981), and *Physical Handicap: A Guide for the Staff of Social Services Departments and Voluntary Agencies* by Lesley Bell and Astrid Klemz (1981), both epitomise this approach. Both books see the matching of needs and services as non-problematic: there are x number of handicapped conditions brought about by y causes; there is a legal and statutory framework, handicapped people have a number of needs and there are these services provided to meet them. Such approaches ignore a number of crucial problems: What is 'need'? Are the services that are provided appropriate? Certainly Bell and Klemz (1981) show little awareness of the ways in which the feelings and aspirations of people with disabilities have changed radically in the recent past.

If only social work with people with disabilities were as simple as this practical approach implies — the matching of resources to needs within a legal and statutory framework. It will be argued here that the dominant view of disability as a personal tragedy or disaster is an inaccurate one and may lead to the provision of inappropriate resources. It will further be suggested that social work as organised professional activity has either ignored disabled people or intervened on the basis of the dominant view of disability as a personal disaster. Chapter 1 will argue this at greater length and suggest a more appropriate theory of disability — what will be referred to as the *social model of disability* — and draw out some of its implications for practice.

This is not to assert the predominance of theory over practice but rather to suggest that there is a symbiotic relationship between the two: that theory will inform practice and orientate the activities of practitioners whose very activities will feed back and modify theory. This view is very close to what Kuhn (1962), in discussing the history and development of the natural sciences, called a 'paradigm'. A sub-title of this book might well be 'The Social Model of Disability — A Paradigm for Social Work'.

Chapter 2 will then consider various ways of conceptualising disability and some of the implications that follow from these different conceptualisations. It will be suggested that the implication stemming from the individual model of disability is to count numbers of disabled people, compile registers, and so on, whereas the social model suggests that ways need to be developed of measuring the disabling effects of the physical and social environment instead.

Chapter 3 will focus on the relationship between impairment and disability in the context of social work practice with individuals, arguing that it is the task of social workers to be primarily concerned with reducing or alleviating the consequences of disability and not the problems of impairment.

Chapter 4 will widen the discussion and consider these issues in relation to social work practice with families where there is a disabled member.

Chapter 5 will consider the role and functioning of residential and day-care facilities and will suggest that, by and large, these services further disable impaired individuals. Suggestions as to how social work can attempt to prevent this imposition of additional disability will also be discussed.

Chapter 6 will consider the legal framework within which services are provided for disabled people, including the rights that disabled people have to access to such services.

Chapter 7 will pull together some of the issues raised in connection with the relationship of theory to practice and consider the implications both for service provision and professional practice that the social model of disability raises. Finally, some consideration will be given to ways forward into the 1980s.

In conclusion, it is important to note that, by adopting such a broad conceptualisation of social work practice, generalisations are made throughout which may not be acceptable to all and which may be in direct contradiction to the experiences of some. My only excuse is that in undertaking what is in fact the first enterprise of its kind in the English-speaking world, I had no well-trodden path to follow or broad shoulders upon which to stand. I was aware that almost every chapter could have been a book itself and thus many issues are treated superficially. I can only hope that having pushed aside some of the undergrowth, that others, social workers and disabled people, will begin to tread the path, though I would not claim broad shoulders for those who follow to stand on!

1

Social Work and Disability: Old and New Directions

Prior to 1970 help for handicapped people and their families was really only available through the health service (medical social workers) or voluntary organisations such as the Invalid Children's Aid Association and the Spastics Society. A few local authority health departments set up professional social work services in the 1950s, staffed mainly by medical social workers and in some cases occupational therapists as well. Welfare departments in the pre-Seebohm days also offered services to the physically handicapped, but as most did not employ trained social workers little was done beyond material help, information-giving, while some provision was made for residential care. However, the Seebohm Report, local government reorganisation and the Chronically Sick and Disabled Persons Act 1970 was supposed to change all that and usher in a new era. Just what this has meant as far as social work with disabled people is concerned will thus be a major theme of this book.

The role of social services departments

In considering the development of services for physically disabled people the Seebohm Report will be taken as the starting-point. While some, notably Brewer and Lait (1980), would argue that this is the wrong place to start, the framework proposed by Seebohm does highlight a number of areas of concern that can be usefully considered.

The Seebohm Report recommended the development of services for the physically handicapped in seven directions as follows:

1. Services for the physically handicapped are in urgent need of development.
2. A reasonably accurate definition of the size and nature of the multiple and complex problems of physical disability will require extensive research.
3. The social service department should be responsible for social work with physically handicapped people and their families, the provision of occupational therapy, residential and day centres for them, holidays, home helps, meals on wheels, sitters-in service, help with adaptations to houses and flats.
4. Substantial development is particularly required in the services for handicapped school leavers, and more thought and experiment is required to determine the best timing and methods of giving guidance on careers to physically handicapped children and young people.
5. Co-ordination of services for physically handicapped people requires a major effort in teamwork. It is impracticable at present to specify a particular form of organisation designed to achieve this everywhere.
6. The emphasis from the point of view of the social service department must be on helping the handicapped individual in the context of his family and community, and for this purpose a broadly based training and approach will be required.
7. It will be quite impossible for local authorities to run effective services for physically handicapped people without help from voluntary bodies.

(Seebohm Report, DHSS, 1968)

Based on Seebohm, the Local Authority Social Services Act 1970 established social services departments in their present form, and its recommendations on physical handicap were incorporated into an additional Act, the Chronically Sick and Disabled Persons Act 1970. Unfortunately this Act was passed at a time of organisational upheaval and there were also the competing demands of other client groups, notably children, who had also been the beneficiaries of recent legislation. The consequence of this has been that while the expectations of disabled people were raised, the new generic departments have been unable to provide adequate support services either in terms of practical aid or emotional support (see Topliss and Gould, 1981; Knight and Warren, 1978; Shearer, 1981b).

If consideration is given to each of the Seebohm recommendations separately, it is possible to make some reasonable estimate of progress in the last few years. Certainly in terms of recommendation 1 services have been developed, though there is still a long way to go. As one study has noted:

> Despite the substantial development of services for handicapped people and the considerable increase of expenditure on these services . . . there were widespread indications . . . that even the most active departments could develop their services further.
>
> (Knight and Warren, 1978, p. 70)

Recommendation 2 suggested that a reasonably accurate picture of the size and nature of the problem should be ascertained, and this was built into the Chronically Sick and Disabled Persons Act as a legal requirement. While all local authorities have conducted their own surveys, the question of accuracy remains. Most of these surveys only located approximately 50 per cent of the people that the government's own survey (Harris, 1971) suggested there might be. In addition many of the surveys are now out of date and this obviously affects their accuracy. Warren *et al.* (1979), in following up their original survey in Canterbury, found that 13.4 per cent of the cohort had died, 4.9 per cent had left the district and 5.1 per cent were in hospital or residential care on a permanent basis. In addition they found considerable changes in the needs of people in their cohort, some needing more help and others needing less. And of course this study did not consider people who had become disabled in the meantime. It is obvious, therefore, that it is an extremely complex and time-consuming business maintaining an accurate picture of the needs of disabled people in a particular area. Indeed some have questioned the allocation of resources in this way, arguing it would be more productive to spend money on direct services rather than counting heads or updating registers.

With recommendation 3 the Seebohm Committee placed the onus on social services departments to provide a wide range of services, foremost among these being a social work service for disabled people and their families. Few, if any, departments would claim to provide such a service. Other services such as residential and day care are often criticised, not on grounds of the failure to provide, but rather in terms of what is actually provided — often 'segregated warehouses'. Durrant suggests that this is a defensive approach and that 'the large gymnasia-like buildings masquerading as day centres, and the purpose-built hostels which advertise the differentness from the rest of the street, typify this approach' (in Brechin *et al.*, 1981). Yet other services such as occupational therapy, holidays, meals on wheels, aids and adaptations are usually criticised on the grounds of the failure of departments to allocate adequate resources to them and not in terms of the kinds of services they provide.

Recommendation 4 suggested the development of services for disabled school-leavers. This is usually left to the careers service, and at present every education authority in England and Wales employs a specialist careers officer for the handicapped. However, according to Rowan:

In July 1978, 6 per cent of young people under 18 registered as unemployed had been out of work for over 26 weeks, and 2½ per cent for over a year; the equivalent figures for registered disabled young people were 30 per cent and 13 per cent.

(Rowan, 1980, p. 71)

It is not perhaps unreasonable to conclude that given present rates of unemployment the situation is much worse now.

Most social services departments are reluctant to attempt to identify the non-vocational needs of disabled young people for fear of the expectations and increased demands that might be created. At present there may only be two such projects in hand, and one of those is being carried out by the voluntary sector.

Improved co-ordination between services was identified as the fifth Seebohm recommendation. This remains a major problem, as Blaxter (1980) clearly identified and Phelan in his review of Seebohm unequivocally states:

> Effective co-ordination is as elusive as perpetual motion and if truly achieved verges on acquiring that very characteristic but frequently social provisions are either organised without acknowledgement of it or administered within a scope which endeavours to eliminate the need for it. *In services for people with handicaps, where generally co-ordination is required more than anywhere else, paradoxically it is to be found the least.*

(in Cypher, 1979, p. 56, *my emphasis*)

The issue of training, which forms the basis of recommendation 6, was taken up by a Working Party convened by the Central Council for Education and Training in Social Work, whose major finding was encapsulated in its title (CCETSW, 1975): *People with Handicaps need Better Trained Workers.* Their major recommendations were for improved training at in-service, basic and post-qualifying levels, and while the post-qualification sector has almost totally disappeared, the general impression of in-service and basic training about disability is little better now than when CCETSW produced its report. Of course, the introduction of the special option on handicap as part of CSS courses and the considerable number of professionals from social services departments who have taken the Open University Course *The Handicapped Person in the Community* will have improved matters a little.

The final Seebohm recommendation was for closer co-operation between the statutory and the voluntary sector. There have been few, if any, studies of this relationship at local level, though voluntary sector provision extends from residential and day-care services to providing individual volunteers for gardening, driving people to appointments, and so on. Hatch, in his study of voluntary organisations in three towns, found:

> At the local level most of the organisations for the handicapped worked quite closely with the statutory services. Where they did not do so it seemed in the three towns more a result of statutory neglect than antagonism on the part of the voluntary organisation. Within this kind of relationship the voluntary organisations were able to communicate needs, but seldom did they openly challenge the adequacy of existing provision by taking up an active pressure-group role.
>
> (Hatch, 1980, p. 105)

Any attempts to assess accurately progress since Seebohm are obviously difficult, but in the light of what has been said it is not unreasonable to conclude that some progress has been made but there is still a long way to go. It is in the area of social work services specifically that least progress has been made, and in the rest of this chapter some of the reasons why this should be so will be considered before going on to outline some of the exciting possibilities that lie ahead for social work intervention with the physically handicapped.

Social work services for disabled people

Specifically with regard to social work services, the CCETSW Working Party concluded that professionally trained social workers should be used:

(a) to provide personal social work help to the handicapped and their families on an individual, group or residential basis where, in addition to or arising from handicapping conditions, clients experience difficulties of a special nature (e.g. additional internal or external or environmental stress).

(b) to assess, with or without members of relevant other professions, the overall situation and specific needs of handicapped clients and their families.

(c) to provide, with or without the assistance of the remedial professions and vocational guidance staff, care, support, advice and guidance; and to assist whenever possible in the process of rehabilitating those with handicaps.

(d) to advise, supervise and contribute to the training of social service staff on the social work aspects of services for those with handicaps and whenever possible to involve the clients in the process.

(e) to plan and co-ordinate services either alone or with members of other disciplines, initiating plans based on where the client is living, include the domiciliary supportive services and take into account all relevant community aspects.

(CCETSW, 1975)

While this sounds fine in theory, in practice social workers (and especially qualified ones) have had a much more limited role.

There have been a number of studies which have discussed social work in relation to disabled people — none is complementary to social work. For example, Parsloe and Stevenson (1978) found that the level and extent of social work intervention with disabled people is relatively low. Occupational therapists or social work assistants in the main provide most input to disabled people and their families. Goldberg and Warburton (1979) found that social work intervention both lacked depth and fared badly in comparison with work with other client groups. Their study showed that 30 per cent of cases dealt with by the intake team and 47 per cent of long-term cases were problems involving physical disability. Of the total of 659 cases altogether 80 per cent were confined to agency review, with the remainder only being allocated to individual social workers. In contrast while cases with child-care, delinquency and family problems produced 29 per cent of the intake cases and only 22 per cent of the long-term ones, almost all of them were allocated to social workers. These and other studies confirm that disabled people have less access to skilled social work support, for, as the Barclay Committee has noted:

Studies comparing caseloads of social workers of differing seniority tend to indicate that senior social workers and qualified social workers carry proportionately more cases of children in care, families with multiple problems or people with mental handicap or illness, whereas un-qualified, inexperienced or assistant social workers carry proportionately more cases of physically handicapped and elderly people.

(Barclay Committee, 1982, p. 11)

Not only that, but social workers also failed to recognise the potential of working with disabled people, for, as Goldberg and Warburton (1979, p. 93) asked: 'What aims did social workers pursue? In just under three quarters of all the cases that were to remain open the preservation of the status quo was all the social workers hoped for.'

Another study found that social work intervention was even positively harmful, for, as Phillips and Glendinning found in a welfare rights project:

it was clear during the course of the project that infor-mation about other benefits had not been sent in any systematic way to the disabled people involved, and that although they were all known to their Social Services Department they had not received advice and encourage-ment to apply for benefits to which they were entitled. Indeed some people had even been given inaccurate information from social workers which had deterred them from making applications for benefits and caused subsequent financial losses.

(Phillips and Glendinning, 1981, p. 43)

Burgess (1982) writes of a case where, despite regular social work intervention, the disabled client has lost more than £4,000 in unclaimed benefit in the past few years.

Recently the Social Policy Research Unit at the University of York undertook an action research project whereby specialist social work support was provided for just over a hundred families with a disabled child, and the results of this specialist intervention were reinforced and compared with an equivalent number of families who did not have such support. The results, as the researchers concede (Glendinning, 1981), were 'both confusing and disappointing'. Certainly almost all of the families appreciated the personal support given by the specialist worker and agreed that it had made a substantial difference to them. However, there was little or no difference between the two groups on all other outcome measures such as the provision of aids, the take-up of benefits, and so on. These results can be interpreted in a number of different ways but do little to contradict the argument that social work support to disabled people and their families is in general inadequate.

The failure of social workers to develop an adequate theoretical and practice base for their interventions has led to criticisms, notably by disabled people themselves, who have accused social workers of ignorance about handicapping conditions, benefits and rights, failing to recognise the need for practical assistance as well as verbal advice and to involve disabled people in the training process. They have also expressed resentment at being treated on a less than equal basis in the professional/client relationship. In addition while disabled people have therefore been critical of social workers, social workers themselves have often been reluctant to throw themselves wholeheartedly into work with this particular group. Certainly there are a number of reasons for this, which may include the following. First, low priority is given to work with this group and hence there are restricted career prospects for anyone wishing to specialise in this type of work. Second, there is a lack of understanding of the potential of working with this group, for, as one writer puts it:

Many people believe that work in the field of physical disability must be depressing because they have a vision of custodial care and of crippled lives filled with sadness and lost dreams. In actuality, rehabilitation of the physically disabled is especially rewarding because of the potential that exists in human beings in the face of stress, a potential that has seriously been underestimated.

(Trieschmann, 1980, p. xi)

Third, as has already been said, poor teaching about handicap on training courses may mean that workers feel inadequate or incompetent when working with physically handicapped clients. Finally, personal fears about handicap may mean that workers may be reluctant to get involved in what they perceive to be the personal and social consequences of adjusting to a human tragedy or disaster. But the major criticism is that social workers, like *all* other professionals, have operated with inappropriate models or theories of disability, and it is in a sense perhaps fortunate that social work intervention has been so limited up to now. Before going on to consider an appropriate model of social work intervention it is necessary to discuss why the current model is inappropriate. For this purpose the inadequate model will be referred to as the 'individual model' of disability, and this can be taken to include the medical model.

The individual model of disability

The individual model sees the problems that disabled people experience as being a direct consequence of their disability. The major task of the professional is therefore to adjust the individual to the particular disabling condition. There are two aspects of this: first there is physical adjustment through rehabilitation programmes designed to return the individual to as near normal a state as possible; and second, there is psychological adjustment which helps the individual to come to terms with the physical limitations. It is not just that social work had accepted the dominant, individual model of disability which is deeply embedded in social consciousness generally, but also that the struggle for professional status and acceptance has also been involved: 'In a search for professional status, social work has emphasised a medical, psychotherapeutic, individualised model of work because that seemed the best way of asserting its expertise and professionalism' (Wilding, 1982, p. 97).

It is possible to be critical of both these aspects of adjustment, and it is the latter which will be focused upon, as it is of most relevance to social work, though there have recently been criticisms of the former also (Brechin and Liddiard, 1981). In order to criticise the psychological adjustment assumptions based on the individual model of disability, spinal-cord injury and blindness will be the disabilities from which evidence will be drawn, though similar points can also be made about other disabilities.

Starting from the assumption that something happens to the mind as well as to the body, a number of psychological mechanisms of adjustment have been identified, or more appropriately borrowed from other areas such as death and dying. Disabled individuals are assumed to have undergone a significant loss, and as a result depression may set in. In order to come to terms with this loss, a process of grieving or mourning will have to be worked through, in similar manner to those who must mourn or grieve for the loss of loved ones. Only when such processes have been worked through can individuals cope with death or disability.

Some writers have seen these mechanisms as a series of stages or steps which have to be worked through. A study by social workers (Weller and Miller, 1977) in New York University Hospital identified a four-stage process by which newly disabled paraplegics come to terms with their disability:

STAGE 1   SHOCK. The immediate reaction to the physical and psychic assault of spinal-cord injury often characterised by weeping, hysteria, and occasionally psychosis with hallucinations.

STAGE 2   DENIAL. A refusal to accept that complete recovery will not take place.

STAGE 3   ANGER. Often projected towards those physically active around them who serve as constant reminders of what has been lost.

STAGE 4   DEPRESSION. A realistic and most appropriate response to a condition of severe and permanent disability and a necessary stage if adjustment, rehabilitation and integration are to be achieved.

Thus the social work task is to help disabled individuals through these adjustment stages.

Albrecht (1976) characterises this and various other

schemes as developmental models and argues that they all, at least partially assume that:

(a) an individual must move sequentially through all of these stages to become fully socialised;
(b) there is but one path through the stages;
(c) an individual can be placed clearly in one stage by operational criteria;
(d) there is an acceptable time frame for each stage and the entire process;
(e) movement through the system is one way, i.e. the system is recursive.

It is not just in the case of spinal-cord injury that such models are considered appropriate, for there are certainly similar ideas in the area, for example, of blindness. According to Caroll (1961, p. 11), 'loss of sight is dying. When in the full current of sighted life blindness comes on a man, it is the end, the death, of that sighted life.'

In order to come to terms with this death Fitzgerald (1970) identified four distinct phases in the typical reaction to the onset of blindness: disbelief, protest, depression and recovery. And indeed these become models for professional practice. For example, a young newly blinded girl was told by a social worker in hospital that she could not have adjusted properly to her blindness as she was not depressed enough. Subsequent social work intervention was thus based on the need to work through this (non-existent) depression despite the fact that the girl involved was more concerned with problems about whether she would be able to continue in her job as a teacher, whether she would be able to continue to live alone and what aids she might need.

There are a number of general criticisms that can be levelled at individualistic theories or explanations. First, these theories implicitly picture the individual as determined by the things that happen to him or her — the adjustment to disability can only be achieved by experiencing a number of these psychological mechanisms or by working through a number of fixed stages. Second, adjustment is seen as largely an individual phenomenon, a problem for the disabled person, and as a consequence the family context and the wider social situation are neglected. Finally, such explanations fail to accord with the personal experiences of many disabled people who may not grieve or mourn or pass through a series of adjustment stages.

Further, it is not just those with spinal-cord injury who question such models. Clark, who lost his sight as a result of a war injury, states:

> The loss of sight need not and usually does not touch the core of a man's intellect and emotional being. What has changed is his relationship with the external world, a relationship with which he had grown so familiar that he scarcely thought of it.
>
> At this stage the very words we use about blindness become a little dubious. It is of course right to describe a war casualty as having been 'blinded', because the word conveys an idea of the violence of the event. Thereafter, however, he simply thinks of himself as lacking the visual sense images to which he had formerly been accustomed. It is something negative that has to be allowed for. He may at times refer to himself as being 'blind' so as to conform with verbal habits of the rest of the public. But privately he does not think of it in that way. Only when he falls into the pattern of ideas that others have of him, does he feel of himself as being 'in darkness'.

(Clark, 1969, pp. 11–12)

Despite these criticisms, it would be true to say that these theories have made up the dominant, individual model of disability and this in itself needs to be explained. A major factor in this is that these theories are in accord with 'the psychological imagination' in that theorists have imagined what it would be like to become disabled, assumed that it would be a tragedy and hence decided that such an occurrence would require difficult psychological mechanisms of adjustment. However, the psychological imagination may not be an appropriate starting-point for such theorising or research — it is surely a value-judgement to assume that disability is a tragedy rather than that it is a phenomenon which may be explained in a number of ways. In the following chapter different meanings associated with disability will be discussed in more detail.

Another factor is that these explanations, being individualistic, are thereby politically convenient. When a disabled person fails to internalise the rehabilitation goals set by the professionals or persistently pesters his local social services department, he can be characterised as having problems in adjusting to his disability. This conveniently leaves the existing social world unchallenged; the goals of the rehabilitator remain unquestioned and the failure of the welfare department to provide the right assistance can be ignored.

While these and other factors may explain the adherence to these psychological theories, they do not explain why these theories have been empirically validated by a number of studies. In fact these theories may become self-fulfilling in at least two ways. At a methodological level, having conditioned research in the sense that they posit adjustment to disability as a problem, researchers then ask questions relevant to that problem and get answers which are then presented as findings, valid social facts. There have been few, if any, studies which started out with the assumption that disability was not a problem. The following quote nicely illustrates the point:

Reflection on the many problems to which the cord injured person must make an adjustment impresses one with the gravity of the psychological processes which occur following cord injury.

Such an individual is confronted with grieving over his loss, coping with pain and phantom sensations, alternations in sexual functioning, loss of bladder and bowel control, the frustrations of immobilisation, loss of vocational goals and earning capacity, feelings of uselessness, role reversals in the family and the attendant loss of self-esteem and the social stigma of being 'different' in the public eye. *It is an amazing tribute to the flexibility and magnificence of the human spirit that so many people whose lives are thus devastated survive*

*and function at the level of physical and social indepen-
dence which most cord injured people achieve.*

(Ibbotson, 1975, p. 5, *my emphasis*)

This quote accurately reflects the process of 'sanctification'
of disabled people which is deeply embedded in the social
consciousness and reinforced through stereotyped media
presentations. There is a polar opposite of this image which
presents disability as a tragedy and personal disaster. As
Shearer suggests:

The 'norm' demands that people whose disabilities are
obvious and severe must be at least 'sad' and even 'tragic'.
And if that defence breaks down in the face of individual
reality, it is ready with its own flip-side. The reaction of
people who break out of the mould becomes: 'Aren't
they wonderful?'

(Shearer, 1981a, p. 21)

In view of these images it is understandable that social workers
are reluctant to get involved, for the scope of professional
intervention with super-heroes or tragic victims must appear
somewhat limited. However, the basic point remains: instead
of questioning social reality with regard to disability, researchers simply proceed on the basis of taken-for-granted
everyday meanings. But as so many paraplegics and blind
people are able to function at a reasonable level, it is surely
more logical to assume that this is a normal everyday reaction.
To put the matter simply, adjustment may be normal and not
a problem at all. And yet with the honourable exceptions of
Shearer (1981a) and Finkelstein (1980), there have been few
studies which start from the assumption of disability as
normality.

There is a second way in which these theories may become
self-fulfilling in that they may actually create the reality they
purport to explain. In the case of mental illness it has been
shown that psychiatrists impose their own definitions of the
reality of particular problems upon their patients. Similarly
in the study of criminal behaviour it has been shown that

criminals will often verbalise theoretical explanations picked up in sessions with psychiatrists, psychologists and welfare workers as excuses for their behaviour even in compulsive crimes like pyromania, kleptomania and child molesting. With regard to disability, many disabled people will have contact with the theories described above, not through meeting academic psychologists or participating in research projects, but through the everyday contact with professional workers who are also internalising these theories. Professional journals are beginning to disseminate these theories widely. An article in *Occupational Therapy* (Ibbotson, 1975) argued not only that individuals must experience the phases of shock, denial, turbulent aggression and working through, but also that there are a number of adaptations that patients must make, including adaptations in body-image, adaptation in role-image, loss of security and loss of self-esteem. A practising social worker expressed the following sentiments:

> Patients must be allowed to come to terms, they must grieve and mourn for their lost limbs, lost abilities or lost looks and be helped to adjust to their lost body-image. Personally, I doubt if anyone who has not experienced the onset of irreversible disability can fully understand the horror of the situation.
>
> (Dickinson, 1977, p. 12)

Finkelstein, himself disabled, has argued that the use of such concepts is nothing less than the imposition of standards of able-bodied normalcy upon the meaning of disability for disabled individuals, partly engendered by the 'helper/helped' relationship:

> The attitude that a disabled person has 'suffered' a personal loss is a value judgment based upon an unspoken acceptance of the standard being able-bodied normalcy. But attributing loss to disabled people is not just the whim of certain helpers. The existence of helpers/helped builds into this relationship normative assumptions. 'If they had not lost something they would not need help'

goes the logic 'and since it is us, the representatives of society doing the help, it is this society which sets the norms for the problem solutions'.

(Finkelstein, 1980, p. 17)

What is being suggested is that the psychological mechanisms and processes that research has identified and described are themselves the product of that research activity both as a result of its methodological predispositions and the spread of this knowledge to professionals who are then able to impose this definition of reality upon their clients. This is beautifully captured by Trieschmann, who asks:

> Is it possible that some of the publications that professionals have written reflect the requirement of mourning? Have professionals seen more stress and psychological difficulty than actually is present? Have professionals uncritically applied terms and theoretical concepts from the field of 'mental illness' to describe the 'normal reaction to an abnormal situation' which onset of spinal injury represents? Have professionals been describing phenomena that do not exist? Have professionals in clinical interactions placed disabled persons in a 'Catch 22' position? If you have a disability, you must have psychological problems: if you state you have no psychological problems, then this is denial and that is a psychological problem. And because this is so, have psychologists, psychiatrists, social workers and rehabilitation counsellors lost credibility with other rehabilitation personnel and with persons who have spinal cord injury, and rightly so?

(Trieschmann, 1980, p. 47)

And it is not just a matter of losing faith but, as she points out, disabled people 'have felt victimised by professionals who write articles about the reactions to spinal cord injury that are based more on theory than fact' (Trieschmann, 1980, p. xii).

Despite these criticisms, it is clear that the individual model remains the dominant one with regard to disability and it has perhaps taken on the attributes of what Kuhn (1962) has called a 'paradigm' — that is, a body of knowledge to which all those working in the field adhere. However, the same writer has shown that paradigms are sometimes replaced or overthrown by 'revolution', and this revolutionary process is often sparked by one or two criticisms of the existing paradigm. Only then can a new paradigm develop to replace the old. Having provided one such criticism, it is now worth considering what a new paradigm — a 'social model' of disability — might look like.

A social model of disability

This new paradigm involves nothing more or less fundamental than a switch away from focusing on the physical limitations of particular individuals to the way the physical and social environments impose limitations upon certain groups or categories of people. Shearer captures the need for this change in paradigm in her criticism of the International Year of Disabled People:

> The first official aim of the International Year of Disabled People in 1981 was 'helping disabled people in their physical and psychological adjustment to society'. The real question is a different one. How far is society willing to adjust its patterns and expectations to include its members who have disabilities, and to remove the handicaps that are now imposed on their inevitable limitations?
>
> (Shearer, 1981a, p. 10)

Adjustment within the social model, then, is a problem for society, not for disabled individuals.

For some, however, it is not just a matter of society's willingness to adjust its patterns and expectations but one of removing the social oppression which stems from this failure to adjust. One statement of this comes from the Union of Physically Impaired Against Segregation (UPIAS), who state:

In our view, it is society which disables physically impaired people. Disability is something imposed on top of our impairments by the way we are unnecessarily isolated and excluded from full participation in society. To understand this it is necessary to grasp the distinction between the physical impairment and the social situation, called 'disability', of people with such impairment. Thus we define impairment as lacking part of or all of a limb, or having a defective limb, organism or mechanism of the body: and disability as the disadvantage or restriction of activity caused by a contemporary social organisation which takes no or little account of people who have physical impairments and thus excludes them in the mainstream of social activities. Physical disability is therefore a particular form of social oppression.

(UPIAS, 1976, pp. 3–4)

While both Shearer and UPIAS are advocating a social model of disability, there are differences in their views which need to be acknowledged. Shearer is asking society (i.e. able-bodied society) to remove the disabilities imposed upon impaired individuals, whereas UPIAS argue that such disabilities will only be removed by disabled people themselves engaged in active 'struggles'. Thus the former sees the reduction or removal of disability as something which may be given, whereas the latter see them as having to be fought for. There are obviously different implications for professional practice stemming from these views, which can be encapsulated in asking professionals whether they wish to work for disabled people or with them. (I am grateful to Frances Hasler for this particular insight.)

This social model of disability, like all paradigms, fundamentally affects society's world-view and, within that, the way particular problems are seen. If the problem of housing for disabled people is taken as an example, the individual model focuses on the problems that disabled people encounter in terms of getting in and out, bathing, access to the kitchen, the bedroom, and so on. In short the approach focuses on the functional limitations of individuals in attempting to use their own environment. The social model, however, sees disability as being created by the way housing is unsuited to the needs of particular individuals. Thus we have 'housing disability'. A housing research project in Rochdale (Finlay, 1978) attempted to operationalise this concept by taking as given the 'reduced performance capabilities' of particular individuals and measuring instead the restrictions that unsuitable housing environments place upon the individuals concerned. The implications of this approach for professionals involves a switch in emphasis away from the provision of personal aids (most of which are not used in any case) and remedial therapy and a move towards adapting environments so that they do not unduly restrict people with functional limitations.

The longer-term policy implications of this approach centre on

> whether the policies most suited to their needs should adopt a preventative approach, in the form of more suitable housing provided in the community, or a remedial approach in the form of para-medical support provided either in the home or special institutions by people whose very intervention, if made unnecessarily, is by itself a disabling factor in the lives of physically handicapped people.
>
> (Finlay, 1978, p. 15)

The same perspective can provide important insights in other areas: the well-known problems of finding out about benefit entitlements are examples of 'information disability' (Davis and Woodward, 1981). Davis and Woodward go on to argue that it is not just the physically impaired who suffer from information disability but

> for those such as people who are physically impaired, where access to specialist information is crucial to meaningful participating, there is a significant distinction. Information disability is a specific form of social oppression. In practice, it results in the disadvantage or restriction of activity caused — not by the impairment

of the individual — but by the way in our society we present, or withhold, information and prevent opportunity for full participation in the mainstream of social life.

(Davis and Woodward, 1981)

When applied to the world of work the social model of disability provides equally valuable insights:

The world of work (buildings, plant, machinery, processes and jobs, practices, rules, even social hierarchies) is geared to able-bodied people, with the objective of maximising profits. The growth of large-scale industry has isolated and excluded disabled people from the processes of production, in a society which is work centred.

(Swain, 1981, pp. 11–12)

This is crucial in capitalist society, where individuals are judged upon what they do and appropriate social status thereby accorded. Hence it is not difficult to see that the dominant social perception of disabled people as 'dependent' stems not from their inability to work because of their physical limitations but because of the way in which work is organised in modern industrial society.

According to Finkelstein (1980), this social model of disability may be most appropriately applied to physical impairments, but it can also take in sensory impairments. For example, deaf people may be disabled by the increasing use of the telephone, which restricts people who can communicate perfectly adequately at a face-to-face level, or meetings may be held in badly lit rooms, so that they cannot adequately see other participants and follow their lips. Similarly, mental handicap can be seen as less the problem of the intellectual impairment of certain individuals but more related to general expectations about levels of social competence. As Dexter wrote more than twenty years ago:

In our society, mental defect is even more likely to create a serious problem than it is in most societies because we make demonstration of formal skill at co-ordinating meanings (reading, writing and arithmetic) a requirement for initiation into adult social status, although such skills are not necessarily related to the capacity for effective survival or economic contribution.

(in Boswell and Wingrove, 1974, p. 294)

The importance of this social model of disability is that it no longer sees disabled people as having something wrong with them — it rejects the individual pathology model. Hence when disabled people are no longer able to perform certain tasks, the reasons are seen as poor design of buildings, unrealistic expectations of others, the organisation of production or an unsuitable housing environment. This inability does not stem therefore from deficiencies in the disabled individual. As Finkelstein (1980, p. 25) points out, 'The shift in focus from the disabled person to the environment implies a shift in the practical orientation of workers in the field.' What does this mean for social work? It is this question which will now be briefly considered.

The social model and its implications for social work

The social work profession has failed to give sustained consideration to physical disability either in terms of theory or practice, and evidence for this view can be sustained by comparing the number of books that have been written about the subject with, say, the number written about children. There have been none solely devoted to the topic of social work and physical disability, and while this is only one example of social work's lack of sustained interest, it is nevertheless a powerful one. This is certainly so when one considers that in recent years social workers have been very keen to write about a whole range of other topics from sex therapy to community work, from children and families to death and dying, from juvenile delinquents to the mentally ill.

However, as was suggested earlier, it is perhaps fortunate that there has been this lack of sustained interest, for social work has adopted the wrong model of disability. The outlining of a social model of disability in the last section before now going on to discuss some of its implications for social work practice goes against the current conventional wisdom which suggests that theory should be practice-based rather than the other way round. Nevertheless to rely on practice to inform theory when practitioners may have already internalised an inappropriate model is to invite disaster, for it would merely result in reinforcement of the individual model of disability at a theoretical level. Therefore, an attempt has been made to lay the theoretical base before considering some of the practice implications. This discussion will inevitably be brief, for it is for practitioners themselves to work out, in conjunction with their disabled clients, the full implications, and not for academics to extract practice blue-prints from their theories.

If consideration is given to the three main social work methods, it is possible to make a number of statements relevant to practice. For example, the switch from an individual to a social model of disability does not signify the death of casework. Rather, it sees casework as one of a range of options for skilled intervention. It does not deny that some people may grieve or mourn for their lost able body but suggests that such a view should not dominate the social worker's assessment of what the problem may be. Blaxter cites one such example of

> Mr. Miller, a young family man with a progressive disabling disease, went to seek the advice of a social worker about his problems, which he was defining in entirely practical terms. In particular he wanted a confused social security position clarified. He returned a little bewildered: 'I don't really know what was going on. I just wanted these forms filled in. She kept on talking about the disease — what I felt about it — what the wife felt about it. Coming to terms with it. All I want to come to terms with is these forms!'
>
> (Blaxter, 1980, p. 123)

Thus grief work or bereavement counselling may be appropriate in some cases but not in all or even most. Some disabled people, particular those suffering from progressive diseases, may need long-term support of the kind that only a casework relationship can provide, and building upon the idea of the disabled family, the whole family may indeed become the target for casework intervention.

Similarly, groupwork need not focus solely on the need to create a therapeutic environment in which individuals or families can come to terms with disability. Groups can also be used to pool information on particular benefits, knowledge on where and how to get particular services, and even on a self-help basis to give individuals the confidence to assert that their disability does not stem from their physical impairments but from the way society often excludes them from everyday life. In addition the group can be used as the major means of giving disabled people back responsibility for their own lives, as is described in a discussion on residential care: 'meetings in the small residential groups were a forum for staff and residents to plan their activities and to determine priorities. They gave the opportunity for residents to take responsibility for themselves and also for the staff to do "social work"' (Dartington *et al.*, 1981, pp. 52–3).

The potential for intervention using community work methods is also exciting. There have already been a number of local access groups which focus on the way the physical environment disables people and numerous access reports and guides have been produced. A few community workers have organised 'forum' meetings of all organisations of and for disabled people in a particular locality and these have proved useful in confronting local authorities about cut-backs, in ensuring that the needs of disabled people are taken into account in pedestrianisation schemes, and so on. And if the definition of 'community' is expanded beyond its strictly geographical meaning to take in the idea of moral communities (Abrams, 1978) or psychic communities (Inkeles, 1964) or what the Barclay Committee (1982) more recently referred to as 'communities of interest', then it is possible to see community work methods being used in disability organisations. For example the Spinal Injuries Association employs a welfare officer whose job is one of enabling its members to work out their own problems and solutions by utilising the collective wisdom and experiences of its 3,000 paraplegic members through mutual support, peer counselling and the provision of information and advice.

In suggesting that theory should inform practice with regard to physical disability rather than vice versa, a number of developments in social work practice compatible with the social model of disability have obviously been ignored. There have undoubtedly been initiatives by individual social workers or departments which are not based on the individual model and which are indeed perfectly compatible with a social model of disability, but social work as a profession has not given systematic attention to developing a theoretical perspective on disability. Such theory has been developed elsewhere, notably by disabled people and their organisations. As a consequence theory and practice have proceeded separately and have not merged into what was earlier called a 'paradigm' in respect of the individual model. It is crucial, however, that in future there is a merger between theory and practice in order to create an alternative paradigm to the one based on the individual model. Only then will the social model replace the individual one, which has proved so ineffective in meeting the needs of disabled people and so unattractive to professionals working in the field.

Conclusions

To conclude this critical overview, it has been suggested that the track record of social work involvement with disabled clients has not been good. Social workers have either ignored disabled people and their needs, or when they have been involved their interventions have been based on inappropriate assumptions about the nature of disability. Certainly social work has failed to develop its theory and practice in terms of even the Seebohm view of seeing the disabled person in the context of family and community, let alone taking on board the implications of a fully developed social model of disability. There are of course reasons for this. Social work, like all other professions, has been unable to shake loose from the individual model embedded in social consciousness generally. It is also of course politically convenient to have the problem located in the individual — repeated requests for assistance can be explained away as signs of having a 'chip on the shoulder' or of a 'failure to adjust to disability'.

The social model of disability has in recent years been articulated not just by individual disabled people but increasingly by a number of disability organisations. For, as Finkelstein suggests:

Disabled spokesmen and spokeswomen have become increasingly active in articulating their own perceptions of their situation. Since the Second World War there has been a rapid growth in the numbers and size of organisations of disabled people and increasingly, particularly during the past decade, a growing group identity.

(Finkelstein, 1980, p. 1)

It is possible to identify three distinct approaches adopted by these groups: the incomes approach, the self-help approach, and the populist approach. All of these approaches, to a greater or lesser extent, build upon the social model of disability, and such activities are likely to be consolidated in the next few years, thereby further exposing the contradictions between the individual and social models of disability.

The time has now come for the professions themselves to join with disabled people and their organisations, and in this social work is ideally placed to play a crucial part. It is less tied to the individual model of disability than the medical and paramedical professions and it has a range of methods of work, skills and techniques which are well suited to working within the social model of disability. The rewards for social workers will arise from the enhanced professional and personal satisfaction that will stem from both the increased range of tasks in which to exercise professional skills and the greater potential for achieving change. In working with disabled people the social work task is no longer one of adjusting individuals to personal disasters but rather helping them to locate the personal, social, economic and community resources to enable them to live life to the full.

In the following chapters some of the themes developed here will be pursued in relation to issues concerning social work practice. It should be re-emphasised, however, that this does not mean that what follows will be a practical manual on 'how to do social work with disabled people within the social model of disability'. Rather, it will be an orientating perspective enabling social workers to develop their practice in conjunction and partnership with their disabled clients.

2
Thinking about Disability

A major theme of this book is that social work, as an organised professional activity, has given little thought to the problems of disability, and where it has it has merely reproduced current thinking in its application to social work practice. A second theme of this book is that much of this current thinking about disability is inaccurate and incorrect at least in that it is incongruent with the personal experiences of many disabled people. A third theme will be to develop more appropriate thinking about disability and to draw out some of its implications for the practice of social work.

There are three main sources upon which to draw when considering the question 'What is disability?' There is social consciousness generally, there are professional definitions of disability and there are personal realities, as articulated by disabled people themselves. Each of these sources needs to be considered separately.

General views of disability

It has already been suggested that the now dominant view of disability is one of personal tragedy or disaster. However, this is not true of all societies, and some may regard disability as a sign of being chosen, of possession by God or the devil. In short, disability does not have meanings which are similar in all cultures, nor indeed within the same culture is there always agreement about what disability actually is. As two anthropologists have noted:

A class of persons grouped together under the term 'physically handicapped' is at best difficult to treat as ethnological data. Here for us is a category of persons with social liabilities peculiar to the conditions of our society. It represents no logical or medical class of symptoms. For example, carrot-colored hair is a physical feature and a handicap in certain social situations, but a person with this characteristic is not included in this class. Nor is the symptom itself the only criterion, for though the person afflicted with infantile paralysis may limp as a result of the disease and be deemed to be handicapped, yet the person with an ill-fitting shoe or a boil on his foot who also limps will be excluded.

When one introduces the concepts of other cultures than our own, confusion is multiplied. Even assuming the existence of such a class in other societies, its content varies. The disfiguring scar in Dallas becomes an honorific mark in Dahomey.

(Hanks and Hanks, 1980, p. 11)

Variations in cultural views of disability are not just a random matter, however, but differences may occur as a result of a number of factors, some of which have been identified by the same two anthropologists:

The type of economy is a factor with its varying production units, need for manpower, amount of surplus and its mode of distribution. The social structure is important, whether egalitarian or hierarchical, how it defines achievement, how it values age and sex.

(Hanks and Hanks, 1980, p. 13)

The type of economy is obviously an important factor in this variation: restricted mobility is less likely to be a problem in an agricultural society than in a hunting and gathering one. And, as has already been suggested, the way production is organised also has implications for 'the speed of factory work, the enforced discipline, the time-keeping and production norms — all these were a highly unfavourable change from the slower, more self-determined and flexible methods of work into which many handicapped people had been integrated' (Ryan and Thomas, 1980, p. 101).

The social structure and values of a society are also important in shaping cultural views of disability. A hierarchical structure like Britain's, based upon values of individual success through personal achievement, inevitably means that most disabled people will be low in the hierarchy on the basis of their reduced ability to compete on equal terms with everyone else. Societies whose central values are religious may well interpret disability as punishment for sin or possession by the devil, or as a sign of being chosen by God.

These and other factors shape social attitudes to disability. The point is that the general view of disability as a personal disaster, an individual tragedy, is culturally specific to Britain and not necessarily the only view. Certainly the view of disability as a personal disaster is a common one in modern industrial societies but there are considerable variations in professional conceptions of disability and their implications for the provision of services and for professional intervention. Scott (see Douglas, 1970) has clearly demonstrated this in his analysis of blindness in the USA, Sweden, Britain, Italy and France. The rest of this chapter is concerned with the way this general view is translated into professional conceptions of disability in Britain and the implications of this for social work.

Current professional definitions of disability

Brechin and Liddiard (1981) have suggested that there may be as many as twenty-three different professionals involved with a disabled individual, though they do not, of course, all use different definitions. Townsend (1979) has suggested that these definitions can be divided into five broad categories: abnormality or loss, clinical condition, functional limitation, deviance, and disadvantage. No single one of these is right or wrong, but rather they are developed for specific purposes or situations, and all can be criticised on various grounds.

(1) *Abnormality or loss.* This may be anatomical, physical or psychological loss, it may refer to loss of a limb or part

of the nervous system or of a sense modality (e.g. deafness or blindness). The existence of either may not necessarily be handicapping. Someone who has lost both legs may well have a very hectic social life, whereas someone else with a minor facial blemish may never go out because of it.

(2)   *Clinical condition*. This will refer to diseases or illnesses which alter or interrupt physical or psychological processes. Arthritis, epilepsy, bronchitis and schizophrenia are examples of such definitions. Diagnosis, however, is often difficult with conditions like schizophrenia or epilepsy, and the government has been involved in controversies over whether a number of ex-miners have bronchitis or pneumoconiosis. If they have the former, they are not entitled to compensation; whereas if they have the latter, they are. Mental handicap is another difficult area, for there is often no clinical diagnosis but rather attempts to assess social competence, or possibly measure IQ.

(3)   *Functional limitations of everyday activities*. This refers to the inability, or at least restricted ability, to perform normal personal or social tasks such as washing and dressing, doing the shopping, negotiating steps or going to the cinema. There are obvious difficulties in establishing objective standards against which abilities can be measured and which take account of other factors such as age, sex and motivation. External factors are also important: someone in a wheelchair in a non-adapted house may be limited functionally, but not in an adapted one. Additionally this definition often leads to the debatable assertion that 'we will all be disabled one day', in that everyone becomes functionally limited by the ageing process. This is normal and expected and while various professional definitions may regard many old people as disabled, it does not follow that they themselves, or society at large, agree with this definition.

(4)   *Disability as deviance*. There are two separate aspects of this that need to be considered: first, deviation from accepted physical and health norms; and second, deviation from behaviour appropriate to the social status of particular individuals or groups. In seeing disability as deviation from particular norms, the problem arises in specifying what those norms are and who defines them. A similar problem arises with regard to deviant behaviour: Who specifies what normal

and appropriate behaviour are, and with reference to what? Deviation from behaviour appropriate to the able-bodied or behaviour appropriate to disabled normality?

(5) *Disability as disadvantage.* This refers to the allocation of resources to people at specific points in the social hierarchy, and in the case of disabled people they often receive less than their able-bodied counterparts. This broadens the concept of disability considerably, for it is not just those with physical impairments who are socially handicapped — so are illiterates, alcoholics and one-parent families, plus, perhaps, racial minorities and women.

Thus there are a number of definitions of disability, none of which presents the whole picture or is the right answer, for, as Townsend puts it:

> Although society may have been sufficiently influenced in the past to seek to adopt scientific measures of disability, so as to admit people to institutions, or regard them as eligible for social security or occupational or social services, these measures may now be applied in a distorted way, or may not be applied at all, or may even be replaced by more subjective criteria by hard-pressed administrators, doctors and others. At the least, there may be important variations between 'social' and objective assessments of severity of handicap.
>
> (Townsend, 1979, p. 688)

In the remainder of this chapter functional definitions will be considered in more detail, particularly in view of the fact that functional definitions are currently the ones upon which access to social services departments and the services they provide usually depend.

Functional definitions of disability

There have been various piecemeal attempts to gather statistics about disabled people, beginning with the census of 1851 which asked questions about the blind and deaf. However, these questions were dropped in 1921 and no census since then has attempted to gather information about disability, largely on the methodological grounds that it is too difficult to frame appropriate questions in such a general survey.

More recently legislative measures like the Disabled Persons (Employment) Act 1944 and the National Assistance Act 1948 required that registers be kept, but only for those in receipt of services, not as any systematic attempt to estimate numbers and establish needs. By the 1960s it was obvious that there were little data available to facilitate the expansion of services for disabled people as part of the general programme of increased welfare expenditure. Accordingly, the then Ministry of Health instigated a research programme which was to culminate in the mammoth study by the Office of Population Censuses and Surveys (Harris, 1971; Buckle, 1971) whereby nearly a quarter of a million households were surveyed. From this survey 8,538 households were followed up and interviewed in depth.

Functional assessments of disability were used in the study and were based on a threefold distinction as follows:

1. *Impairment*: 'lacking all or part of a limb, or having a defective limb, organ or mechanism of the body'.
2. *Disablement*: 'the loss or reduction of functional ability'.
3. *Handicap*: 'the disadvantage or restriction of activity caused by the disability'.

The measurement of extent of handicap was based on a series of questions regarding people's capacity to care for themselves. The response to each question was graded according to whether the activity could be managed without difficulty, with difficulty, or only with help. Some activities were regarded as more important than others and measurements were weighted accordingly. The most important items were:

(a) getting to and using the toilet
(b) eating and drinking
(c) doing up buttons and zips

Other items were:

(d) getting in and out of bed
(e) having a bath or all-over wash

(f)   washing hands and face
(g)   putting on shoes and stockings
(h)   dressing other than shoes or socks
(i)   combing and brushing hair (women only)
(j)   shaving (men only)

The responses to these questions were collected, and as a consequence disabled people were divided into four categories: (i) very severely handicapped, (ii) severely handicapped, (iii) appreciably handicapped, and (iv) impaired. According to this functional measurement, it was estimated that there were 3,071,000 impaired people, or 7.8 per cent of the total population. In terms of the categories of handicap, Harris estimated the following numbers in each category:

Very severely handicapped	157,000
Severely handicapped	356,000
Appreciably handicapped	616,000
Impaired	1,942,000
	3,071,000

The Harris survey also highlighted two other important facts: that handicap increases with age; and that disabled women begin to outnumber disabled men in the older age groups (Tables 2.1 and 2.2).

Table 2.1   *Proportion per 1,000 of men and women in different age groups, in private households in Great Britain, with some impairment*

Age group	Proportion per 1,000 with impairment		
	Men	Women	Men and women
16–29	10.0	7.9	8.9
30–49	30.2	25.6	27.9
50–64	85.6	84.6	85.0
65–74	211.4	227.1	220.7
75 and over	316.2	409.0	378.0
All ages	66.7	88.2	78.0

Source: Harris (1971 p. 5).

Table 2.2   *Estimated numbers of men and women in Great Britain, in different age groups, living in private households, who have some impairment*

Age group	Estimated number in Great Britain		
	Men	Women	Men and women
16—29	50,000	39,000	89,000
30—49	197,000	170,000	366,000
50—64	401,000	433,000	833,000
65—74	356,000	559,000	915,000
75 and over	243,000	625,000	867,000
All ages	1,247,000	1,825,000	3,071,000

Source: Harris (1971, p. 4).

Overall there are considerably more disabled women in the population than there are disabled men, but within the age structure there are significant variations. In fact up to the age of 50 both in sheer numbers and prevalence more men are likely to be defined as disabled than women. Two possible reasons are: (i) many more men work and risk disablement through accidents and work-induced illnesses, and (ii) many more young males partake in dangerous sports and leisure activities, e.g. motor-cycle riding, rugby, mountaineering, etc. Consequently these figures reflect sexual divisions within society whereby certain activities, both work and leisure, are dominated by males. After the age of 50, then, not only are there more disabled women but their prevalence in the population is also greater. This is a reflection of the fact that women live longer than men, coupled with the fact that prevalence of a significant number of disabling conditions increases with ageing. Additionally, of course, functional definitions of disability use measures of physical capabilities, and as these inevitably decline with ageing more and more elderly people are defined as disabled.

The Harris study has formed the basis for much subsequent thinking about disability and has played an important role in the planning and development of services. However, there are a number of important criticisms that can be levelled.

Townsend has suggested that the Harris study adopted too narrow a definition of disability and therefore grossly under-estimated the numbers of disabled people in the population: 'disability itself might be best defined as inability to perform the activities, share in the relationships and play the roles which are customary for people of broadly the same age and sex in society' (Townsend, 1979, p. 691). In operationalising his broader definition in his massive survey of poverty he concludes that there are three times as many handicapped people as Harris suggested. Table 2.3 illustrates the differences in numbers produced by these two surveys.

Table 2.3   *The disabled in Britain: two national surveys*

Harris (1971)		Townsend (1979)	
Degree of handicap	Total numbers	Degree of incapacity	Total numbers
Very severe	161,000	Very severe	325,000
Severe	366,000	Severe	780,000
Appreciable	633,000	Appreciable	1,990,000
Minor	699,000	Some	3,915,000
No handicap	1,297,000	Little or none	2,890,000
Total	3,146,000	Total	9,900,000

There are two points of clarification that need to be made. First, the Harris figure of 1,297,000 individuals with no handicap refers to people who have impairments but are not handicapped, at least according to this particular definition. Second, the Townsend figure of 2,890,000 people with little or no handicap includes 180,000 children between the ages 0–9. Children were specifically excluded from the Harris survey.

The figures produced by Harris have not always proved reliable in estimating the cost of introducing new benefits nor indeed do the figures always match with data collected

by government for other purposes. According to Jaehnig
(in Boswell and Wingrove, 1974, p. 449, n. 2), upon the
introduction of the attendance allowance it was estimated
from the Harris survey that there were approximately 25,000
people entitled to it — yet in the first year alone there were
more than 72,000 successful applicants. And Topliss points
out:

> From the government survey in 1969 it was estimated
> there were 697,000 impaired men and women in the
> labour force or temporarily off sick or actively seeking
> work. Only 176,000 of these were classified as substan-
> tially handicapped by their impairments. On the other
> hand, there were in 1978 over half a million names on
> the Disabled Persons Employment Register, kept by the
> Employment Services Agency, and yet it was thought
> that only one third of those eligible to register in fact
> were registered. This would suggest that there are
> substantially more than the estimated 697,000 impaired
> people in the work force.

(Topliss, 1979, p. 48)

She goes on to suggest that this discrepancy is 'undoubtedly
due to the different definitions of disability employed', in
that many people who may have few or minor functional
limitations may nevertheless be severely handicapped in
obtaining employment.

Functional definitions are still not acceptable to all, and
Finkelstein suggests that these definitions still locate the
causes of disability at the level of the individual, whereas
'The cause of handicap lies within the society which disadvantages impaired people . . . handicap is caused by having
steps into buildings and not inability to walk' (in Finlay,
1978, app. 7). Finkelstein then proposes a reversal of the
Harris terminology along the following lines:

> Firstly, that the cause of handicap lies within the society
> which disadvantages impaired people by taking no, or
> very little account of their physical condition and

consequently does not provide the solutions, for example providing ramps for wheelchair users who are unable to walk up steps . . . Secondly, I suggest changing the definitions of the words *handicap* and *disability* around. In this way a person is disabled when he or she is socially prevented from full participation by the way society is arranged.

(in Finlay, 1978, app. 7)

While there are very real and important criticisms of the Harris work, it did at least attempt to obtain the extent of the problems of disability looked at in a coherent and systematic way. Unfortunately, while the Harris survey recognised the social dimension of disability, it still attempted to utilise what remains an individual measure and to locate the problems of disability within the individual.

While the results of the Harris survey were being published, the Chronically Sick and Disabled Persons Act was making its way through Parliament. Its very first section stated:

It shall be the duty of every local authority having functions under section 29 of the National Assistance Act 1948 to inform themselves of the number of persons to whom that section applies within their area and of the need for the making by the authority of arrangements under that section for such persons.

So it was not just a matter of counting heads but also of making provision to meet need.

The main reason for including this section was not merely to identify the numbers of handicapped people in particular local authority areas, for that could have been done by reference to the Harris survey which had analysed its data in this fashion, but rather to identify each disabled individual in a particular area. As Topliss and Gould (1981, p. 90) put it, 'There can be no doubt, therefore, that the original intention of Alf Morris was that local authorities should identify, person by person, the handicapped individuals in their respective areas.' However, under guidance from the DHSS, local authorities were directed towards making assessments of numbers rather than attempting to identify specifically every disabled individual. All local authorities have now complied with this duty either by carrying out house-to-house surveys, sample surveys or using other methods.

Knight and Warren have summarised the findings of these surveys and suggest:

> Most of the CSDP [Chronically Sick and Disabled Persons Act] surveys found that the crude prevalence rate for all impaired and handicapped people living in the community was from 40 to 70 people per 1,000 of the population of all ages, i.e. from 4% to 7% of the population were found to be physically impaired. Between one third and one half of these were handicapped, i.e. experienced significant disadvantage, in one way or another, by their impairment and just over one tenth (or nearly 1% of the whole population) were very severely or severely handicapped. The presence of impairment and handicap increased markedly with age. Fewer than 1% of the population aged less than 16 years were impaired, about 3% of those aged from 16—64 years, about 18% of those aged from 65 to 74 years and from 40% to 50% of those aged 75 years or more. It follows from this that the majority of disabled people are elderly and many are very old and, because of the longer life of women compared to men, most disabled people in the older age groups are women (after the age of 75 years two thirds or more of disabled people are likely to be women).

> (Knight and Warren, 1978, pp. 68—9)

From this it will be seen that these surveys provide a picture of handicap, at least in terms of age structure, gender and severity of disability, at the local level which is broadly similar to the national picture found by Harris. However, in numerical terms, the numbers of disabled people on local authority registers in England in 1980 was 900,669. Thus it is clear that social services departments have located only one in three disabled people, at least according to the Harris estimate of numbers.

Nowhere in the Chronically Sick and Disabled Persons Act 1970 was the idea of a register mentioned, but as the keeping of a register of disabled people was made a requirement of the National Assistance Act 1948, many local authorities decided that keeping one was the way to meet their duty under section 1. As Phelan (1979) puts it, 'Section 1 was hailed as the master key to social provision for people with handicap.' There are problems in keeping registers, however. First, some people may feel that inclusion on a register is an invasion of privacy and may be stigmatising. Second, it is difficult to keep registers up to date and in line with changing circumstances and capabilities of those registered. Finally, as has already been pointed out, Warren *et al.* (1979) showed that registers are likely to be extremely inaccurate (by up to 30 per cent or more). The most telling criticism of registration, however, is that there is only a tenuous link between it and the provision of services. The following situation is described by Topliss and Gould:

> None of the services for handicapped individuals is conditional upon the recipient being first recorded on a local authority register. Neither is the entry of a person's name on the register any guarantee that he or she will receive any service at all. It is true that more of those who are registered are in receipt of services than those who are not registered, but this is chiefly because application and receipt of a service identifies a person as handicapped and his or her case is then recorded. In other words, it is the fact that a service has been asked for and given that leads to entry on the register for many disabled people, rather than the other way round. There is certainly still a good deal of ignorance on the part of disabled people about services provided by the local authority for which they may be eligible, but merely registering a person as disabled does little or nothing to broaden his knowledge of services that could assist him. The dissemination of information to disabled people about services can be, and usually is quite independent of any register.

> (Topliss and Gould, 1981, pp. 100—1)

Finally, then, the criteria for registration offers considerable discretionary powers to those doing the registering, both in terms of the resources available in a given area and the personal whims of those undertaking the registration process. Satyamurti found examples of this:

> Criteria for registration were laid down, but these criteria left a certain amount of room for interpretation which made it possible for there to be a considerable degree of variation in practice, both between individual social workers and, probably more importantly, between area teams, as to the kind of criteria laid down. Other teams, however, took as their criteria not so much the characteristics of the client concerned, as considerations about what services would be available to that client if he/she were registered, which would not otherwise be available. Thus in Area X, for instance, it was common practice for social workers to register clients, particularly the elderly, as physically handicapped on such grounds as shortness of breath or arthritic pain, in order that they could then arrange for the client to have a holiday to which otherwise he/she would not be entitled. Social workers would vie with each other in a joking way as to how little in the way of physical impairment they could get away with.
>
> (Satyamurti, 1981, p. 37)

Leaving aside these criticisms, the problem of registration for social work, particularly when viewed from a social model of disability, is a false one. It starts from the assumption, built into the Chronically Sick and Disabled Persons Act, that *all* disabled people have special needs and that statutory provision should be made to meet them. The resource implications of such a view have become apparent and need not be dwelt upon here. However, it is the assumption that all disabled people should be identified in order to meet their needs that is false.

It has been variously estimated that perhaps as many as three in four disabled people may not wish to be known to social services or have any needs that statutory provision might meet. One study, based on a survey of Remploy employees (Owen, 1981), found that only 40 per cent of those interviewed had actually used the services of a social worker. Given that registers appear to identify only one-third of disabled people, it is clear that the idea of providing a comprehensive service for all disabled people has proved unattainable. In addition the underlying assumption locates the problem within the individual and fails to take into account the way the physical and social environments impose handicaps upon impairments. Services are therefore geared to the problems of individual limitations rather than to alleviating the restricting effects of physical and social environments. Social services departments and social workers, then, most of whom have regarded registration as a crucial issue, have in fact been operating in the wrong area. Phelan makes a clarion call to social workers:

> Transform the war memorial of Registration into a roll of honour, put it on display and have a page turned daily to a fanfare of trumpets. For the benefit of citizens with handicaps let us explode the myth of registration, exploit its meaning and clear the way for counting to lead to caring.

> (Phelan, 1979)

The social work task in this particular area is thus not to identify and register impaired individuals; it is rather (i) to identify ways in which disabilities are imposed upon impairments with a view to remediation, and (ii) to provide a flexible and accessible service to meet such individual needs as may arise. It is for planners and policy-makers, not social workers, to identify the likely extent of such needs. Of course, some will say that this is all very well, but central government at present allocates funds to local authorities on the basis of head counts, but there is no reason why local authorities should not suggest that this is an inappropriate way to proceed, and that alternative ways of estimating and meeting needs should be explored. Sutherland, for example, suggests that new definitions of disability need to be developed:

The most useful basis for such a definition is the fact
of stigmatisation itself. If we make no attempt to
create a definition based upon some type of physical
incapacity, but simply define this group as consisting of
all people who are stigmatised or discriminated against
on the basis of their physical condition, we have an
extremely practical rule of thumb definition.

(Sutherland, 1981, p. 20)

Whether a definition based on stigma would prove adequate
is perhaps debatable, but it is certainly clear that any definitions need to move away from personal physical incapacity
or functional limitation as their base-line.

Self-definitions

It is not just individual disabled people like Finkelstein and
Sutherland who are articulating different definitions of
disability, but a growing number of disability organisations
are also beginning to demand the right to define the problems
faced by their own members. More will be said of this later
but it is worth noting at this point that the inaugural meeting
of Disabled People's International, a congress representing
disabled people from over fifty countries, recently rejected
the *International Classification of Impairments, Disabilities
and Handicaps* (World Health Organisation, 1980) on the
grounds that it was too closely allied to medical and individual
definitions of disability.

Self-definitions are not only important at the level of the
disabled individual. Professionals have often been reluctant
to accept a disabled person's own definition and have used
terms like 'denial' and 'disavowal' to account for contradictions between definitions. The assumption that has usually
followed from this is that it is the disabled person who is
mistaken or misguided and the professional who is correct.
It logically follows from this perception of a given situation
that the social work task is to facilitate a more realistic assessment of the situation by disabled persons themselves.

What in practice this may amount to is the social worker imposing the professional definition upon the disabled person, and it is certainly true that the only way to gain access to certain benefits and services is to 'act disabled'. However, as Blaxter's study showed, in situations where professional and self-definitions conflict, this was much more likely to give rise to long-term problems than when these definitions were in accord: 'One of the circumstances in which the problems of adjustment and rehabilitation were very likely was when the patient's own view of his condition differed from that of his doctors' (Blaxter, 1980, p. 221).

The problem for professionals generally, and for social workers in particular, is not working out the correct or right definition of disability, for part of the argument here is that there is no such thing. Definitions depend upon a number of factors, some of which have already been identified and some of which have not. Albrecht and Levy argue that definitions of disability are socially constructed and such social construc- tions often reflect vested professional interests:

> Certainly it is in the interest of medical professionals, hospitals, nursing homes, and medical supply companies to find treatable, chronic disabilities. Yet, the disabilities identified, discovered, and treated may reflect pro- fessional and occupational exigencies rather than actual consumer need. For these reasons, *disabilities can be seen as socially constructed entities regardless of their physiological bases.*

> (Albrecht and Levy, 1981, p. 21, *my emphasis*)

Thus social workers need to recognise that disability is a social construction and not necessarily a fixed physical entity, and need to plan their strategies of intervention accordingly. Some of the ways in which they might do this are considered in following chapters.

3
The Causes of Impairment and the Creation of Disability

The distinction between individual and social dimensions of disability already referred to are also important in discussing the causes of both impairment (individual limitation) and disability (socially imposed restriction). From an individual/medical view the main causes of impairment can be seen from Figure 3.1 on page 52.

Following this line, Taylor suggests that this approach is entirely justified in that the major causes of impairments are diseases of various kinds. It follows from this that 'Unlike the case of most instances of mental handicap, there is a significant medical contribution to be made within the overall pattern of support for physically disabled individuals' (Taylor, 1977, p. 10). In short, most disabling conditions are caused by disease, doctors cure diseases, and even where they cannot cure medical intervention will often control symptoms. Therefore, doctors have an important, if not crucial, role to play. The question of the relevance of medical knowledge for social work intervention will be discussed later in the chapter.

In the meantime it is sometimes argued that these diseases are 'residual'; and that their increased incidence is a result of two factors, increased life expectancy and the growing numbers of elderly people in the population. A consequence of this view is the assumption that these diseases are 'degenerative' and largely a product of the age structure of the population. According to Doyal:

The new 'disease burden' consists largely of the so-called 'degenerative' diseases, such as cancer, heart disease, arthritis and diabetes, all of which now kill and cripple many more people than they did in the past. In 1975, approximately 26 per cent of deaths in Britain occurred from cerebrovascular disease, 20 per cent as a result of cancer, and 4.5 per cent as a result of chronic bronchitis, emphysema or asthma. In addition, of course, many more people are becoming chronically ill for longer periods in their lives than they did in the past.

(Doyal, 1980, p. 59)

The list of diseases causing death and disability here are very similar to the list provided by Taylor, but whereas Taylor sees the prospects of prevention as limited and the medical profession as the appropriate agency for dealing with the causes and consequences of such conditions, Doyal has an alternative view more in accord with Finkelstein's social definition of disability. It could be argued that while Finkelstein suggests that disability has social causes, Doyal sees impairment as having social causes also.

Using the work of Powles (1973) Doyal argues that these degenerative diseases occur almost exclusively in advanced industrial societies and, regardless of their individual causes, they result from the fact that the environment to which humans are biologically adapted has changed fundamentally. The living conditions of advanced industrial societies produce diseases of 'maladaptation'. The implications of this view differ from those derived from the view of Taylor, in that if the causes of these diseases are ultimately environmental (social) rather than individual, then perhaps the medical profession is not the crucial agency that should be involved. In short, if these diseases are the consequence of a dysfunction between human beings and the environment, then it is to the material environment that programmes of treatment (or prevention) should be directed. Indeed, some writers, notably Illich (1975), have suggested that the disappearance of a number of diseases such as typhoid, cholera, polio and tuberculosis is solely due to changes in the material environment

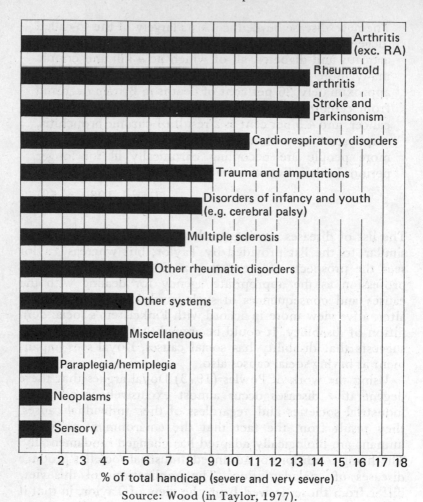

Figure 3.1   *Main causes of severe and very severe handicap in adults of working age (16—65)*

and the role of medicine has been irrelevant or even positively harmful. He develops his argument through usage of the term 'iatrogenesis', by which he means 'doctor-induced illness', which he defines as 'illness which would not have come about unless sound and professionally recommended treatment had been applied'.

Prevention

A major reason for considering the causes of both impairment and disability is that it raises the possibility of prevention. As Albrecht and Levy put it:

> The major causes of mortality and morbidity today — heart disease, cancer, stroke, diabetes and accidents — can be prevented partially by changes in the environment and life-style. That is why the Surgeon General of the United States advocates altered health practices in terms of smoking, overweight, drinking alcoholic beverages, hours of sleep, regularity of eating breakfast, eating between meals and physical activity . . . Disability and the costs of rehabilitation could be partially controlled if those precipitating events that are preventable were eliminated. To avoid blaming the victim, preventative efforts should be directed at the industries and governmental agencies that promote disability-causing behavior rather than by merely faulting those individuals who become disabled.
>
> (Albrecht and Levy, 1981, pp. 26–7)

However, the term 'prevention' as used by the medical profession is not necessarily the same thing as the concept of 'prevention' used by social workers. Leonard (1966) attempted to distinguish between three levels, which he calls primary, secondary and tertiary. For him primary intervention is aimed at preventing the causes of certain events, secondary intervention is aimed at preventing the immediate effects of events, and tertiary intervention is aimed at preventing the consequences of these events. This threefold distinction is very similar to the classifications of disability produced by Harris and Finkelstein discussed in the previous chapter. The ideas discussed so far can be summarised in the form of Table 3.1.

This perspective therefore sees the medical profession and health educators as being largely responsible for primary prevention: that is, reducing the numbers of handicapped babies being born, providing information about the prevention of accidents at work, and so on. Secondary prevention, i.e.

Table 3.1   *Definitions and the scope for intervention*

Professional intervention	INDIVIDUAL MODEL Harris/Wood/Taylor	SOCIAL MODEL Finkelstein	TYPE OF PREVENTION Leonard
Medical profession and health education	Impairment	Impairment	Primary
Paramedics and rehabilitation staff e.g. OTs, physios	Disability	Handicap	Secondary
Social workers, politicians, pressure groups	Handicap	Disability	Tertiary

the reduction of the personal limitations that may be imposed by impairments, falls to rehabilitation staff in particular. Tertiary prevention, i.e. the reduction of socially imposed restrictions upon impaired individuals, forms a large part of the social work task in working with people with disabilities. As Leonard (1966, p. 12) has suggested in respect of social work generally, 'Much of social work has concentrated, necessarily, on tertiary intervention; for example, the intervention involved in the whole field of the care of adults and children in residential institutions, foster homes and hostels.'

Of course, the real world is not as simple as Table 3.1 suggests, and it may be that social workers will be involved at the primary and secondary levels also, in providing ante-natal advice to pregnant clients or in helping to locate the best available rehabilitation services. However, it is the contention here that the social work task essentially falls within the tertiary level and what now needs to be explored further is the range of knowledge and skills necessary to carry out this task.

Medical knowledge and the social work task

One immediate question posed by this conceptualisation of

the social work task concerns the question of how much knowledge of medical conditions social workers actually need. In suggesting that it is the social rather than the individual/ medical model within which social workers should operate, it does not logically follow that they should have no knowledge of medical conditions. Indeed, without such knowledge it may well be impossible to consider the personal, interpersonal or social consequences for the client concerned. Such knowledge may be acquired from other professionals or through reference books of various kinds. *Get Help* by Halliburton and Quelch (1982) is a particularly useful example. However, in most cases the major source of such knowledge is the disabled person. Thus one young social worker, when allocated a female tetraplegic at a case conference, approached her new client by telling her that she knew nothing about tetraplegia but was willing to learn. The worker and client thereby agreed to spend a complete day together from the time before the tetraplegic woke up until after she fell asleep in bed. The social worker learned more about tetraplegia from that particular experience than ever she could have done from books or other sources, and as a consequence was able to provide the client with satisfactory service.

It is important to extract other aspects from the medical facts: whether the condition is visible or non-visible, whether it is static or progressive, congenital or acquired, whether the impairment is sensory or physical, will all have important effects upon the personal, interpersonal and social consequences of particular impairments. Hicks spells this out in the case of visual impairment:

Because of the inabilities to acquire information through sight and to make eye contact with other people, the visually handicapped, and particularly the functionally blind, may encounter relationship and sexual problems which are not common to other disabilities. These problems differ for those whose visual impairment is congenital (from birth or infancy) or adventitious (occurring after some visual concepts have been formed). They apply to initial encounters, to the range of potential partners, to sexual relationships and they have clear implications for education and counselling and for professional relationships with the client.

(in Brechin *et al.*, 1981, p. 79)

What is being suggested, for visual impairment in particular and for all disabilities in general, is that such aspects are more important for the social worker than to know whether the impairment was caused by glaucoma, cataracts or retinitis pigmentosa.

Disability, then, is neither simply an individual misfortune nor a social problem: it is a relationship between the impaired individual and the restrictions imposed upon him by society. This relationship is defined by Finkelstein: 'society disables people with different physical impairments. The cause, then, of disability, is the social relationships which take little or no account of people who have physical impairments' (in Brechin *et al.*, 1981, p. 34). Disability is thus a relationship between individual impairments and the social restrictions imposed by social organisation.

A framework for intervention

For the social worker to utilise this idea of disability as a relationship, some way of linking the individual and the social is needed. One such attempt has been made through development of the concept of 'career', which originally developed in American sociology (Becker, 1963; Goffman, 1963) but later came to be used on both sides of the Atlantic in discussions of disability (Safilios-Rothschild, 1970; Blaxter, 1980). Carver has provided a comprehensive definition of the concept in relation to disability:

A 'career in disability' refers to the course of progress through life of any disabled person insofar as he encounters problems or handicapping conditions related in any way to his disabilities. A person's progress may be affected in relation to his working life, but not his domestic or wider social life — or vice versa — but this would be likely to happen only if the disability were a minor and limited one, since for most people all aspects of life tend to be inter-related. It may be affected in practical ways and/or in the ways he thinks about himself or others. This concept of career is a broadly comprehensive one and implies that the individual is actively and repeatedly involved in the definition of his own problems and in the search for solutions, and like any other career, it will comprise a succession of interactions with his environment, both physical and social. A career in disability may in principle come to an end when all impairment-related problems have been solved; but in the case of enduring disability fresh problems may arise at any time and it is wiser to assume that the individual's career may persist from the onset of disability until the end of his life.

(Carver, 1982, p. 90)

Thus in working with individuals the concept of career provides a link with social structure and offers the social worker the possibility of conceptualising disability as a social relationship. On its own the idea of a 'career' will provide a useful basis for short-term or crisis intervention in that support and help may be needed when a career in disability begins. But for some people with disabilities longer-term involvement may be necessary.

In order fully to make use of the concept of 'career' it needs to be harnessed to the notion of 'life-cycle events': that is, that there are key transition stages in life through which everyone passes, such as birth, starting and leaving school, puberty, going to work, marriage, retirement and death. These transition stages are often marked by uncertainty as individuals move from one role or status to another, and this can give rise to adjustment problems both for the individuals themselves, and for family, friends, peers, and so on. People with disabilities will also move through key life-cycle events, though disability may exacerbate some of the problems involved and enhance the need for professional intervention. For example, anxious parents may well seek to help their disabled offspring at a childhood stage well into the period when the people with a disability feel they should be treated as adults.

From other social scientific research it is possible to predict certain occurrences at particular stages in the life cycle. For example, poverty is more likely to occur when a family is bringing up young children and around the point of retirement; personal relationships are often fraught around the time of puberty; unemployment can be particularly severe during adolescence; and family crises may occur during the early years of marriage when parents are adapting to having young children in the home. It is possible to link together the concepts of 'career' and 'life-cycle events' in diagrammatic form (see Figure 3.2).

The first column provides a chronological listing of the ages at which life-cycle events occur and these events are then listed in the second column. The third column then provides some indication of the kind of events that may occur and the need for intervention. The fourth column plots a number of possible 'disabled careers'. This final column indicates that disability can occur at any particular point in the life cycle, and can also end, sometimes by the provision of a cure, and more often by early or premature death. The point of the diagram is to sensitise the social worker to the 'disability relationship' and the number of possible factors which may be involved. Which of them is important and should serve as a target of intervention will be for the worker, in full discussion with the client, to determine. For example, one disabled woman experienced severe emotional difficulties during her adolescence but the social work support she received was solely geared towards her disability. She now realises that her disability was unrelated to her emotional disturbance, which was part of the normal process of growing up experienced by all girls.

It is necessary now to say something about the applicability of this scheme to the real world of social work practice. With limited resources, pressures on time from other cases, departmental management not sympathetic to this kind of work, and so on, most social workers are unlikely to have the luxury of planning long-term intervention in working with disabled

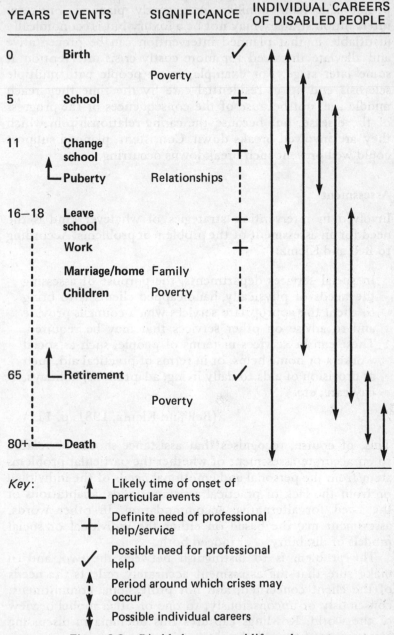

Figure 3.2 *Disabled careers and life-cycle events*

people and their families. A properly planned long-term intervention strategy may not be a luxury but is economically justifiable in that planned intervention can be preventative and alleviate the need for more costly crisis intervention at some later stage. For example, many people with multiple sclerosis end up in residential care by the time they reach middle age, not because of the consequences of the progress of the disease, but because the caring relationship in which they are involved breaks down. Consistent, planned support could well prevent such breakdowns occurring.

Assessment

Involved in intervention strategies of whatever kind is the need for an assessment of the problem or problems. According to Bell and Klemz:

> In social services departments, the purpose of assessing the needs of physically handicapped clients is to bring to them the appropriate services which councils provide and to advise on other services that may be required. These can be services in terms of people, such as social workers or home-helps, or in terms of practical aid, such as provision of aids to daily living, adaptations, holidays, day care, etc.
>
> (Bell and Klemz, 1981, p. 117)

This, of course, recognises that assistance should be related to an accurate assessment of whether the particular problems stem from the personal and emotional needs of the individual or from the lack of practical assistance, aids, adaptations or the need for alternative accommodation. In other words, assessment may be based on either the individual or social models of disability -- or indeed both.

The problem is to distinguish between the two, and to make sure that the assessment accurately reflects the needs of the client concerned, and not professional commitment, consciously or unconsciously, to one or other model or view of the world. Rowlings captures this dilemma in discussing assessments of the elderly:

The . . . identification of the more obvious practical needs should also provide reliable information as to the presence or otherwise of additional emotional or relationship problems for which social work help may be appropriate. Not every client will require or want social work support and certainly the provision of social service should not be dependent upon a social work recommendation. Nor is it feasible or even desirable that every client referred for social service also receives a separate assessment to see if social work help is appropriate.

(Rowlings, 1981, pp. 65–6)

This dilemma is equally true in assessment of disabled people, and testament to the fact that social workers often get it wrong can be found in Shearer:

Understanding is meant to be part of the stock-in-trade of the social worker. They may have plenty of it but little practicality: 'They are all very nice and sympathetic', says one middle-aged woman with cerebral palsy who lives with her now ageing mother. 'They will come and talk for hours. Then they go back and make long duplicated reports and nothing happens unless we keep on and on making a nuisance of ourselves.' Or they may not seem to understand at all. So a man who contacted his local social services office to seek help with getting his ceiling painted was treated instead to a lengthy visit which had to do with the need the social worker saw for him to come to terms with the fact that he had, some years ago, broken his spine. So a woman who quite badly wanted to discuss the particular strains of living with a disability that fluctuated in the restrictions it imposed was treated instead to a bright homily about the different bath aids now on the market.

(Shearer, 1981a, p. 113)

There are at least three problems involved in correct assessment. First, there is the question of who does the assessment. The evidence (Parsloe and Stevenson, 1978) suggests that it is either done by occupational therapists or social work assistants. The problem with OT assessments is that they tend to be based on functional limitations and consequently are more appropriate to the secondary level discussed in Table 3.1 above. Social work assistants, on the other hand, may not have the requisite skills to distinguish between personal and social problems, let alone the relationship between the two. A second problem involves the ethics of assessment and centres on the question of whether or not requests for practical assistance should involve workers in attempting to dig below the surface to see whether the request is merely a presenting problem. A final problem involves the tools and techniques available for assessment purposes, most of which are based upon functional limitation, though in recent years there have been some attempts to measure the quality of the environment: for example, PASS (Wolfenberger and Glenn, 1975) with regard to mental handicap (also discussed in some detail by Anderson, 1982) and the Rochdale Housing Assessment (Finlay, 1978) with regard to housing disability.

A final issue in the discussion of assessment involves the relationship between professional and client and the extent to which the client is able to participate. Brechin and Liddiard outline some of the problems involved:

It can be argued that, in making assessments, professionals are basically gathering information in order to clarify their understanding or model of what is going on in the same way as anyone might. Where there may be a difference is in the extent to which professionals formalise, condense and standardise the information gathering processes. By virtue of their training they have acquired certain pre-constructed models which have been tried and tested already, and these they will attempt to use first to make sense of each new situation.

By the same token, however, in developing a specialised focus, in attempting to maintain objectivity, and in trying to operate economically, professionals have a tendency to narrow the scope of their assessment. The individual involved, on the other hand, may be overwhelmed by an abundance of first hand information regarding all aspects of his/her life experiences and may find it quite hard to disentangle critical factors. If these two assessment procedures could be combined, the possibility of reaching a more balanced view would seem to be considerably increased.

(Brechin and Liddiard, 1981, pp. 38–9)

It would not be appropriate at this point to make detailed suggestions about how assessments should be done, but in conclusion two points need emphasis. Assessments that take account of individual and social aspects of disability and the relationship between them need to be undertaken by competent and knowledgeable professionals taking into account the wishes, concerns and goals of their clients. Most importantly, if the social dimension is included, then it is social workers who need to be involved because they are concerned with the tertiary level of intervention, as outlined above. To finish as the chapter began, the social model needs to be applied to both impairment and disability, otherwise the criticism levelled by Corrigan and Leonard will remain unchallenged:

In the field of physical handicap, for example, symptomatic treatment at the individual level is still the primary response, in the case of bronchitis, structural responses would require a substantial indictment of methods of economic production, in the case of mental disorder, medical models of treatment are still dominant, a dominance which allows the neglect of structural factors in the creation of mental disorders. Poverty itself, and the stigma associated with it, is indissolubly linked in both definition and service delivery to individual pathological conceptions.

(Corrigan and Leonard, 1979, p. 101)

4
Disability in the Family

The social model of disability can be a useful and sensitising perspective in considering the implications of disability for family life. There are three ways in which the 'disability relationship' discussed in the previous chapter is important here. To begin with, disability in an impaired individual may be exacerbated by the way he or she is treated by the family, as with the way some disabled children are overprotected by their anxious parents. In addition family structure and stability may be adversely affected by one of its members becoming disabled, though it is important to note that such an occurrence may strengthen rather than weaken familial ties in some situations. Finally, there is the question of the way society treats families, through social policy provision, where there is a disabled member.

These themes will be interwoven in this chapter, but to begin with it is necessary to consider the consequences of disability within the family and the scope and possibility for social work intervention. To locate the family in its appropriate social context it needs to be recognised that it is a universal social group which in one form or another occurs in all societies and at all times.

In Britain there has been a tendency to overromanticise historical aspects of family life, seeing families in the past as much more capable of looking after their own, particularly weaker, members and coping in times of stress. However, it is sometimes argued that in the past 100 years family size has reduced considerably and the past extended family has become the modern two-generation nuclear family. Also, the family has lost many of its functions to the state, which provides education for all children, care and treatment for sick members and economic support in times of unemployment.

The accuracy of this picture of family life is still the subject of much debate. Some writers have argued that the nuclear family has always been the basic family unit, while others have suggested that there is little evidence to support the notion that the family was better able and more willing to support other family members in the past than it is now — there were more old people in institutions, for example, in 1900 than there are currently. Certainly it is true that there have been a number of very important changes in the nature of the family. First, there has been a rapid increase in marital breakdown; the divorce rate has risen from 2.6 per cent in 1951 to 9.6 per cent in 1975 (per 1,000 married population). Second, and as a consequence of this, there are many more one-parent families, though some are of short-term duration because people re-marry. Finally, the increasing numbers of elderly people in the population at large has placed an additional caring burden on many families.

Young and Willmott (1973) characterised the present-day family as 'symmetrical': that is, where often both the husband and wife work but family life is centred on the home and family members share most of the domestic tasks. Obviously when a disability occurs within the family, this limits the possibility of sharing tasks and may also exacerbate other internal and external pressures on the family. As Topliss puts it:

> Although the precise impact of disablement upon family life depends upon the position within the family of the disabled person, a growing body of literature suggests that whether it is a handicapped husband, wife, child or elderly parent who is affected, disablement has an important effect on the relationship and opportunities of the family as a whole.
>
> (Topliss, 1979, p. 129)

What is being suggested is that in considering the consequences of disability within the family, external economic and social pressures on family life need to be taken account of, as well as the impact of the disability itself upon individual members and the family as a unit. Families with an impaired member may be further disabled by poor housing, poverty, lack of emotional support and the lack of social provision generally.

Children with disabilities

The birth of a handicapped child can be a traumatic and shattering event for a family and that is the dominant way both professionals involved and researchers have treated the subject. As a consequence it has usually been assumed that as well as needing appropriate information and practical assistance parents also need skilled help to overcome the loss, grief and bereavement they feel as a consequence of failing to produce a healthy child. This view is summarised by Selfe and Stow:

> Many writers have dealt with the initial emotions experienced by parents. These often include extreme feelings of shock, helplessness, shame, embarrassment and guilt. In addition there may well be feelings of frustration, and rejection of the child. Some psychologists have seen this as part of the process of grief and mourning for the normal child who was never born. Others conceive parents to be in a state of chronic sorrow because they are faced with the life-long reality of their situation.

> (Selfe and Stow, 1981, p. 205)

However, this view does not pass completely unchallenged, and others have suggested that the birth of a handicapped child does not, of necessity, promote adverse emotional reactions (Roith, 1974), while Baldwin argues that, even where stress is present, it may stem from unresolved practical problems:

> Many writers, particularly those who are themselves professionals or addressing professional audiences, take

as their starting point the assumption that severe disablement in a child has abnormal and pathological effects
upon the family. This approach is often used to justify
professional judgements about the kind of help families
'need'. It can also, as Wilkin [1979, p. 41] argues, lead
to neglect of the practical problems of day to day living.
Above all, it tends to neglect the fact that disabled
children are individuals, bringing their own rewards and
stresses, happiness and disappointments, much the same
as other children. The assumption made here is that
severe disablement almost invariably creates practical
problems. Providing help with these can relieve stress on
families and enable them to function, as far as possible,
like other families.

(in Walker and Townsend, 1981, p. 124)

Thus, in discussing the impact of a handicapped child upon
family life, differing views based upon the individual and
social models of disability once again emerge.

Lonsdale, who carried out her own study, makes sense of
these differing views in the following way:

It is known that some parents cope and some do not,
but as yet we have little explanation of the reasons for
this. It might be that there are links between being able
to manage and having adequate finances, or with enjoy-
ing secure relationships within the family, or with the
nature of handicap itself, or it might be a combination
of all three. The nature of the problems suggest that it
is an area for social work involvement but of what kind
and when it is likely to be most helpful has perhaps
been insufficiently considered.

(in Lonsdale *et al.*, 1979, p. 1)

There are thus at least three areas where social work has
an important role to play: in providing emotional support
when needed, in providing access to practical assistance and
resources, and in reducing the negative impact that dealing

with an unfeeling professionalised bureaucracy may often have. These need to be considered separately.

In dealing with the emotional impact upon the family, it should be stressed that not all families will need professional help. However, for those that do, Jordan, in the introduction to *Children, Grief and Social Work*, which all social workers working with families with handicapped children should consult, issues the following warning:

> Social workers do not 'know the right way' for people to react in such circumstances, still less should they impose their stereotyped formulae on others suffering. Rather they are there to help people find their own way through their crises, and to provide a substitute for or complement to the fellow-feeling once given mainly by the afflicted to each other.
>
> (in Lonsdale *et al.*, 1979, p. viii)

Despite this warning, Lonsdale, in the first paper in the book, is stuck within the individual model of disability and makes recommendations accordingly:

> Handicap and mourning are inextricably linked. The birth of an obviously severely impaired child is often accompanied by a sound of silence followed by sotto voce discussion amongst midwives and doctors and a quick removal and separation of baby from the mother. The mother, and the father if he has been present at the delivery, know that something is wrong. Just how wrong they may have to wait to know, but from that moment a psychological process is set in motion. Parents begin a grief reaction to the loss of something they had been anticipating for nine months or longer, and that is a normal baby. Part of the aim when telling parents is to facilitate the grieving process that follows, and *the main role of the social worker is to help the parents to grieve in a healthy way*.
>
> (in Lonsdale *et al.*, 1979, p. 5, *my emphasis*)

As well as neglecting the practical problems that may arise, Lonsdale is too accepting of the universality of grief processes. At least one writer has cynically suggested that ideas of grieving and mourning may be inappropriately applied to areas other than death, and have been extended largely as a consequence of the paucity of other social work theories:

> Another way of padding the depleted number of deaths in order to shore up the relevance of grief theory is the notion of helping the parents of children born with handicaps to grieve for the perfect child who isn't.
>
> When you come to think of it there isn't much else theoretical which is taught on your average social work method course except grieving and mourning.
>
> (Baird, 1980)

This is not to argue that some parents may not experience a grief reaction, but rather that social work practice should not begin with that assumption. Issues concerning assessment discussed in the previous chapter are equally important in working with families with a handicapped child and the social model of disability may be equally appropriate.

What is absolutely clear is that social workers must adopt a flexible approach and not base their interventions on preconceived ideas or theories. Elfer (in Lonsdale *et al.*, 1979) describes his experiences working with families with a terminally ill child and says that he began with two assumptions: that the child should be told about his illness, and the family encouraged to talk about it. These assumptions were soon lost when he found that help had to be geared, not to normative assumptions about a healthy family life, but to the way in which each family coped. Thus he found that there were few if any ground-rules upon which to structure his intervention and he concluded: 'Perhaps the only one is the importance of offering help quickly — but situations that occur can be so threatening, painful or bizarre that responses have to be those that seem right and appropriate for the situation, however unorthodox' (in Lonsdale *et al.*, 1979, p. 6).

Thus in providing emotional support the appropriate place to start is with the coping strategy of the family itself, and it is important not to see some reactions as pathological and others as healthy. This means that the social worker will often be working in a situation of uncertainty, but better this than attempt to impose a professional definition upon a personal problem.

A second area in which families with a handicapped child may need help is in the area of practical problems. Swain (1981), in his discussion of disability in the family, sees the main practical problems as suitable housing, a reasonable income, reduction of the limitations on mobility that may be caused, and perhaps an increase in time and energy spent on the 'normal' child-care tasks that all parents are required to undertake. He concludes:

In general, however, families with disabled members experience changes in circumstances (including job opportunities and suitability of housing) which can lead to circumscribed resources and increased demands upon time and energy. The functioning of the family depends upon the way they organise themselves and adapt their environment in the face of such changes.

(Swain, 1981, p. 19)

Certainly it can be part of the social worker's job to help in this organising and adapting: in making sure that the family is receiving all the financial benefits it is entitled to, contacting organisations like the Family Fund where necessary and negotiating with other agencies such as housing departments.

A final area where families may need help is in dealing with the stresses created by their dealings with apparently unfeeling professionals and bureaucracies. There is growing evidence that doctors are particularly poor at telling parents about their handicapped child, as Ballard (in Lonsdale *et al.*, 1979) vividly shows in discussing his own experience, while the Collins family (in Brechin *et al.*, 1981) graphically describe the way they were shunted from one place and professional to another with little or no help offered. Robinson (1978), in his discussion of the relationship between professionals and clients with a disabled child, encapsulates his findings in the title of his book *In Worlds Apart*. He identifies a number of dimensions of the problem, including poor communication between the doctor and parents and the failure of professionals to acknowledge, let alone deal with, parental feelings of discomfort or threat. In addition he found that parents felt powerless with regard to decisions made about their child's future and some professionals individually behaved in an autocratic way. Finally, the service offered was of itself inadequate.

Again social workers can be involved in two important ways: first, as members of teams involved in telling parents, they can try to ensure that it is done in the most appropriate and humane way possible; and second, they can provide emotional support for parents who may need to resolve their feelings of anger and distress about the way they have been treated.

In this section on families with a disabled child, the fact that most space has been devoted to emotional reactions of the families concerned does not mean that this is regarded as the most important problem. Rather, it is the problem to which social work has devoted most attention and it is for this reason that it has been considered at length. However, the need for practical assistance may in many cases be paramount and social work assistance with locating and providing appropriate resources may be crucial. This once again suggests a shift in focus, away from the individual model and towards a social model of disability.

Growing up with a disability: making relationships

Certainly many disabled young people experience difficulties in making relationships of either a social or a sexual nature, and there are a number of factors in this, some of which may be related to individual problems and others which may be a consequence of the social and physical environment. Stewart accurately sums this up when he says that

Disabled people sometimes have severe relationship difficulties, either through sheer lack of opportunity for meeting and involvement with other people, or through deficiency in the emotional and social skills which enable adequate development and maintenance of friendships and love affairs.

(Stewart, 1979, pp. 20—1)

Specific aspects of these problems need to be discussed in a little more detail in order to clarify areas where social work intervention may be appropriate.

Disabled people may not have the same opportunity for meeting other people. Many social gatherings, such as youth clubs and discos, may simply be physically inaccessible, and in a wheelchair it may not always be possible to participate in that favourite teenage pastime of hanging around on street corners. Disabled people may also find it difficult to initiate contacts in pubs or at parties. To take the initiative and take a seat close to someone who is attractive may be very difficult for someone in a wheelchair, and for visually impaired people it may be impossible. Parents of disabled youngsters are sometimes overprotective and reluctant to allow their children to take the usual teenage risks. Furthermore, disabled teenagers may also find it difficult to do things that perhaps they should not (when they go out they probably have to be transported by their parents). They therefore can't lie to their parents about where they have been or who they have been with. (I am grateful to Jack Hughes for this particular insight.)

Special schools are often criticised for exacerbating these problems in a number of ways. For a start they usually take handicapped youngsters away from their own home environment and peers for most of the year, and by the time they eventually leave these segregated establishments peer relationships have often been formed in their local community on a lasting basis and they find themselves excluded. Criticism is often levelled at these schools not only in terms of the educational standards they provide but also because they fail to provide remedial social skills programmes to alleviate the negative effects of segregation. These criticisms are very serious when it is borne in mind that nine out of ten handicapped children are still educated in special schools. Hence special education may further disable impaired adolescents.

Another major problem for disabled people in making and sustaining relationships is the reaction of other people. There are two aspects of this. Other people may be prejudiced towards the disabled individual or indeed may simply be uncertain about how to treat him or her — should the disability be ignored, or spoken about openly, and, if the latter, at what stage in the relationship should such questions be raised? On the other hand, disabled people may be unsure or simply lack experience about how to present themselves to other people. This may occur as a consequence of overprotection by parents or segregation during their education. Thus disabled people may be too intense in their personal relationships or may want to move to different stages in a given relationship too quickly. It is certainly clear that other people are a part of the problem, for, as American sociologist Edwin Lemert has commented:

> Although physical handicaps partially restrict opportunities for achievement, the more critically operating limits come from an overlay of interpersonal and formal social barriers founded upon cultural stereotypes about physical defects. As many physically disadvantaged people say, the problem is less the handicap than it is the people.
>
> (Lemert, 1967, pp. 16—17)

Stewart shows how making relationships for disabled people may be more of a problem for disabled young people than for others:

> Our relationships, including our sexual relationships, are formed mainly within our circle of established acquaintances, and the smaller the circle, the less the opportunity. The part which unsuitable ingress to premises plays in limiting social — and hence relation-

ship — activities for handicapped people is incalculable. Admittedly, some disabled people will make use of this excuse to withdraw from social life, but for others it remains the main problem.

(Stewart, 1979, p. 36)

So the main problems involved in making relationships with disabled youngsters are the physical environment, the response of others, segregative educational practices, overprotection and the lack of experience that some disabled people themselves have in coping with the demands of an able-bodied world. Sensitive social work intervention should take account of the possible presence of some of these factors and should encourage disabled youngsters to take their place in the world and not be segregated from it in schools, day centres and residential units.

Sex and disability

The sexual problems of disabled people have received much attention of late. In fact, it could be argued that sexual aspects of disabled people's lives have received too much attention and that they should be returned to where they belong — to people's private lives. Certainly it is true to say that the attention attracted by the 'sex and disability industry' reveals as much about society's own values as it does about the sexual aspects of the lives of disabled people. Once again, then, the individual and social models of disability need to be considered in relation to sex — the individual sexual problems that some disabled people may have (individual model) and value-judgements concerning appropriate and acceptable ways of expressing sexuality in present-day society (social model).

Once again it is Stewart who is most relevant on the sexual problems of individual disabled people. In his own survey he found:

Over half the disabled people interviewed (searchingly and at some length) were found to be subject to current, personal, significant sexual problems: the precise proportion was 54%. A further 18% had experienced such problems since the onset of their disorders (whether at birth or later) but these had become less significant — having been solved by personal effort, infrequently resolved by suitable advice or counsel, all too often fading into insignificance only with time and custom.

(Stewart, 1979, p. 39)

There is little other empirical evidence about whether the proportion of disabled people experiencing sexual difficulties is greater than the rest of the population or not. Stewart's findings also need to be qualified by the fact that the numbers in his sample were fairly small, and as a sexual counsellor it is likely that he would be sensitive to this particular aspect of disabled people's lives. Certainly the assumption made by some professionals that sexual problems are an inevitable problem for disabled people and their partners is unwarranted.

The relevance of this discussion for social work intervention is that it would be wrong to assume that all disabled people have unresolved sexual problems of one kind or another, but that when it is apparent that there are sexual problems it might be useful to have some understanding of possible causes. Pain may be a factor which makes it difficult to achieve satisfactory sexual fulfilment for both parties, as may impotence, depending upon the particular medical condition. Real or imagined physical danger can also affect sexual performance, as can the side-effects of some medication. Incontinence and incontinence devices may also inhibit or affect sexual relations. Finally, it has been clearly established that psychological factors like fear, anxiety and a poor self-image can also adversely affect sexual performance.

It would be foolish to deny that most disabled people are impaired in sexual performance if we take the dominant cultural values of completed coitus and multiple orgasms as the standard. However, that does not imply that it is not possible for the vast majority of disabled people to achieve satisfactory sexual relations. The problem then may be one of social expectations and cultural values rather than impaired individual performance, though of course the discrepancy between social expectations and individual performance may be experienced as personal inadequacy.

The social model of disability may also throw light on the sexual problems of disabled people in day-centres and residential establishments, in that often these problems are in the minds of professionals rather than disabled people themselves. They stem from decisions made about segregating disabled people in particular kinds of institution and the rules made in them to regulate all behaviour, including sexual. That is not to deny that there are genuine moral issues to be resolved concerning issues like helping disabled people to masturbate if they are unable to do it themselves, or putting them in a bed of their choice and not where staff think they should be. These issues are not only related to sex, however, but also to things like smoking cannabis and many other activities. The point is that problems created by able-bodied people organising services in particular ways are often turned around and located at the level of individual disabled people. Hence, were the organisers of a recent conference entitled 'The Sexual Problems of Disabled People in Residential Care' operating within the social model, the conference would have been called 'The Problems Sexuality Creates for the Running of Residential Establishments'.

Disability and marriage

Sex may or may not be a problem in marriages where one or both of the partners are disabled. But certainly there may also be practical problems of housing or mobility, and most of the aids and adaptations are geared to the single person: ripple mattresses are not made in double sizes and extensions to houses are usually only built to accommodate the disabled person, regardless of whether there is a partner or not. Townsend (1979) found that 'half the households with a disabled member had an income at or below the poverty line'. However, what little evidence there is on the break up of marriages where there is a disabled member is conflicting. Topliss (1979) in a survey in Southampton found that 16 per cent of disabled women were divorced or separated compared with a national divorce rate of 7 per cent at the time. However, only 4 per cent of disabled men were divorced. Sainsbury (1970) suggests that marriages are more likely to break up when the wife rather than the husband is disabled. On the other hand, Blaxter (1980) in her study in Scotland found that the divorce rate among disabled men exceeded that among disabled women.

Again, social work intervention should not proceed on the assumption that disability in marriage may create marital problems; even where marital problems are present, they may stem from outside rather than from individual defects. One way of highlighting possible stresses brought about by social expectations is through the concept of 'role'. When sociologists talk about roles, they usually mean 'behaviour oriented to the patterned expectations of others' (Merton, 1957). This then provides the link between the individual and social structure and suggests that people's behaviour takes account of social expectations, and failure to behave, or to be able to behave, in this way may create stress and conflict.

Where the husband is disabled, he may not be able to behave in the roles expected of him, particularly in the sphere of work, and hence his economic role may be affected. On the other hand, where the wife is disabled it may have less effect upon her role performance. To say this is not to be sexist in making inappropriate assumptions about role performances based on gender but to recognise the reality of the situation where, while seven out of ten housewives may go out to work, considerably less than 50 per cent of disabled married women in fact do so. Blaxter's study makes a similar point:

> There was much evidence about the strain which impairment can put upon marital relations. This seemed more likely in the case of the husband's disablement than the wife's, though it may be only that wives were more willing to talk about it. In only a few cases did a wife's disablement cause a complete change in the family's way of life, however (when, for instance, the husband had to give up his work to care for her); for the most part the wife 'managed', with varying degrees of hard-

ship, with formal or informal help of other women. A husband's disablement, on the other hand, meant a radical change; he might have to stay at home and adjust to 'idleness', or change his job or conditions of work, which affected the whole family pattern.

(Blaxter, 1980, pp. 203–4)

People do not perform roles simply based on external social expectations but each individual marriage may produce its own internal expectations about the roles for each partner. Whether disability occurred before or after marriage can then be an important factor in 'role strain' within a marriage. This can best be explained by examining Table 4.1. The usefulness of this table is that it can be used to sensitise workers to the disability relationship implicit in the social model of disability in that it focuses upon the links between individual impairment, family structure and social expectations.

Table 4.1   *Marriage, disability and role relationships*

Disabled before marriage	Disabled after marriage
1. Husband	2. Husband
3. Wife	4. Wife
5. Husband and wife	6. Husband and wife

1. No change in internal role structure.
2. Husband may have to give up his economic role and wife may be forced to be main wage-earner.
3. No change in internal role structure.
4. Husband may be forced to give up his job, though wife may still be able to be homemaker.
5. No change, but practical problems of day-to-day living may predominate.
6. Changes most likely to be part of ageing process and therefore can be accommodated gradually. However, the person becoming disabled first may often adopt the 'cared-for' role with the other partner taking the role of 'carer', regardless of the eventual extent of impairment of each partner.

Disability in marriage may thus give rise to three kinds of problems: individual problems of a personal or sexual nature, problems related to lack of resources or practical provisions, and, linking the two, discrepancies between individual behaviour and social expectations. Social work assessments will need to take account of the possibility of any or all of these factors being present in order to avoid the situation described by Blaxter (1980, p. 219) where 'Social work support for emotional and family problems tended to be available only after a crisis situation had developed, when help might be too late.' But again social workers should avoid assumptions that any or all of these problems must be present. In many marriages where there is a disability no help may be needed at all. Shearer quotes one description of what is an entirely 'normal' marriage:

> My wife goes about her daily chores. I earn the living; we have friends who accept us; our bungalow is indistinguishable from the neighbouring bungalows except that possibly ours is a little better kept. My wife helps me to dress; I help her to bath; we have sexual intercourse frequently; we row about my driving; she never has enough housekeeping money; she always lacks something to wear for the special occasion; in fact, it's all very normal.

> (Shearer, 1981a, pp. 29–30)

Growing old with a disability

Any consideration of disability has to take into account that, by adopting a functional definition, the majority of disabled people are in fact old. It is not the intention to deal separately with the topic of social work with elderly people, for this has been covered by Marshall (1983) and Rowlings (1981). Rather, the effects upon the family of having a disabled elderly relative living within it need to be looked for.

A recent study by the Policy Studies Institute (Nissel and Bonnerjea, 1982) found that the economic cost of caring for an elderly disabled person within the family was £8,500 a year when both the cost of financial benefits available and loss of earnings are taken into account. Further, it is clear that most of the emotional, psychological and physical burdens of this caring usually falls on one person, the wife in the family. As one reviewer has commented:

> An important finding is that, once the elderly person has moved in, caring is no longer seen as a shared activity. Siblings disappear, children give (and are not usually expected to) no help and the neighbourhood offers nothing. Biological ties are superseded by perceptions of women's work by the husband, as he offers no more help when his parents are involved than when his wife's parents are the dependants. Teenage children don't bring friends home; husbands disappear to work and the pub. A picture of isolation and family breakdown comes into focus.
>
> (Oliver, J., 1982, p. 477)

While the number of families in this study were small, another larger survey (Equal Opportunities Commission, 1982a) estimates that more than a million women are involved in similar caring relationships.

Even if the caring is only done by one person, it is not hard to imagine the stress and strain that such situations place upon all relationships within the family. This has led to a number of key demands being advanced by carers to alleviate the situation (Oliver, J., 1981). These demands include a twenty-four-hour community nursing service, as existing services are often too inflexible to be of much use to many families. To supplement this it is suggested that more Crossroads care-attendant schemes are set up as they are the only schemes specifically designed to offer support to the carer. Another demand is for more temporary and phased care facilities and for better publicity to be given to those younger disabled units and other residential units which offer such a service. The need for information for carers about resources, facilities and services is as important as for disabled people, for they are just as likely to suffer from 'information disability' (Davis and Woodward, 1981). A key demand is for financial recompense and a recognition that carers are saving vast sums of money, for residential care is a very costly alternative for the state. One specific aspect of this issue which is patently unjust is the fact that married and cohabiting women are not entitled to the invalid care allowance, whereas single women, and indeed all men, are entitled to claim this benefit.

These demands for extra resources show that it is not only the person concerned who may be disabled by his or her impairment but the carer may also be disabled by it. There is also a considerable emotional burden to caring for a disabled relative, often for many years and shouldering the burden alone. Thus a final demand of carers is for understanding:

> Many of the respondents said that they welcomed any opportunity to talk with someone who understood what they were going through. (They also said that this was often only possible when they were able to speak outside the presence of the disabled person — hence many a 'doorstep interview'). In order to try and fulfil this need, and others, an Association of Carers is being formed. It is envisaged that this will be a two-tier structure — local branches to establish local needs and resources and offer individual and group support, and a national 'umbrella' organisation to feed information down to the branches and act as a pressure group on government.
>
> (Oliver, J., 1981, p. 19)

It is clear that social work has a role to play both in providing additional resources and meeting the emotional needs of carers. However, there is also potential ground for conflict over who the social worker might regard as the client. The elderly handicapped person, the carer or the family as a whole all have claims to such status, particularly where the needs of each potential client are different and possibly conflicting themselves. And indeed, one of the main criticisms of social workers by carers is that they usually adopt too narrow a focus and perhaps neglect the wise words of Alf Morris, formerly Minister for the Disabled, that 'a disabled person almost invariably means a disabled family'. There are no easy answers to such conflicts except to say that skilled and sensitive intervention should always balance the needs of all parties concerned, even though all the parties may not all be the client. Only in that way can the needs of the client be met at all satisfactorily.

In drawing together all the issues raised in this chapter, the words of Swain seem most apposite:

> Summing up . . . we might say, with Farber [1975] that 'in most respects these families resemble others in society. Most of their roles and values are drawn from and are sustained in a flow of events similar to that experienced by other families.' This statement . . . holds true when we look at processes of development in families with disabled members of any age. Perhaps the evidence can best be summarised as showing that a disabled person (whether child or adult) does not create unique diffi-culties for the family, but rather disability exaggerates, or highlights, the dilemmas or paradoxes which are an inherent part of family life in our society.
>
> (Swain, 1982, p. 30)

5
Living with Disabilities

In the previous chapter disability within the family was discussed, but there are a number of disabled people who do not have families, or do not wish to continue to live with their families, or indeed whose families are not prepared to accept them at home. Despite the development of some care-attendant schemes and the Community Service Volunteers (CSV) 'One-to-One' project, when this situation occurs the only option often available to the disabled person is residential care:

> In Great Britain we have a habit of providing for 'difficult' minority groups in segregate institutions and those suffering traumatic tetraplegia are no exception. It is a tradition which has roots in the Poor Law and which comes down to us today virtually unchanged. Only rarely can someone who depends heavily on others for personal help, and who for some reason does not have the support of — or wishes to live independently of — his or her family, find an alternative system of accommodation and care.
>
> (Davis, in Brechin *et al.*, 1981, p. 322)

Usually there will be little choice about whether or not to go into residential care and very little chance of opting for one type of care rather than another. It is interesting to note that the most common reason for disabled people entering residential care is family break up or the refusal of the carer to continue with his or her tasks. The severity of the impairment or the progressive nature of the medical condition are much less important. Thus for many people living alone with a disability, the institution is where they will probably end up.

Residential care for all client groups has been heavily criticised in recent years and this is equally true in respect of disabled people. From the perspective of the social model of disability, there is little doubt that the experience of residential care further disables impaired individuals. However, before going on to discuss this in some detail, residential care needs to be put into its appropriate legal and social context.

It has gradually been acknowledged that the most appropriate place to live with a disability is in the community, even for those people with severe disabilities. Alf Morris, in opening the Sunningdale conference on disability, gave voice to this view when he said that 'Happily more and more people are coming to see that it is undesirable to institutionalise even severely disabled people, that their needs must increasingly be met in the community.' This philosophy has been enshrined in official documents (DHSS, 1976, 1981), and endorsed in reports like the Snowdon Report, and given parliamentary approval through a series of legal measures, notably the Chronically Sick and Disabled Persons Act.

This movement obviously has important ramifications for the shape and future of residential care facilities for disabled people. Some, like the Union of the Physically Impaired Against Segregation, have called for nothing less than the complete disappearance of all segregated and segregative institutions: 'The Union's eventual object is to achieve a situation where as physically impaired people we all have the means to choose where and how we wish to live. This will involve the phasing out of segregated institutions maintained by the State or Charities.' And while stopping short of a demand for closure of all existing institutions, they state that 'The Union is opposed to the building of any further segregated institutions' (UPIAS policy statement, *Disability Challenge*, May 1981). Topliss has argued for the need for additional residential facilities: 'The real issues are the desperate shortage of facilities and the fact that standards and variety in the provision of residential accommodation are not commensurate with expectations and variety of needs of disabled individuals' (in Topliss and Gould, 1981, p. 118).

Before considering the implications of the social model of disability and the possible tasks of social workers in relation to residential care, it is necessary to fill out some of the legal background, outline some of the criticisms of residential care and consider some of the alternatives. It is also worth noting that the numbers of disabled people in such care constitute less than 10 per cent of all disabled people.

This chapter is concerned with disabled people under the age of 65 in residential care. Table 5.1 suggests that there are 76,000 under 65 in residential care; but 55,000 of these are accommodated in mental abnormality hospitals. Thus we need to consider approximately 20,000 who are being accommodated in either private or voluntary homes, local authority homes and young disabled units (YDUs), run by the NHS.

Table 5.1 *The distribution of the disabled population between private households and residential care (including hospitals)*

	No. in private households (a)	No. in institutional care (b)	Total no. of disabled (c)	Column (a) as percentage of (c)
Under age 65	1,453,000	76,000	1,529,000	95.0
Over age 65	1,782,000	267,000	2,049,000	87.0
All ages	3,235,000	343,000	3,578,000	90.4

Source: Topliss (1979, p. 81).

The legal situation

Social services departments have a duty under part III, section 21, of the National Assistance Act 1948 'to provide residential accommodation for persons who by reason of age, infirmity or any other circumstances are in need of care and attention which is not otherwise available to them'. Despite subsequent amendment by the Local Government Act 1972, the statutory duty remains.

The 1948 Act recognised a powerful historical tradition for charitable agencies to be involved in such provision and thereby permitted local authorities to delegate their powers to approved agencies if they so wished. Some authorities chose to do this, and the largest agency providing residential accommodation for disabled people is the Leonard Cheshire Foundation, which has a network of over seventy Cheshire homes throughout Britain. The NHS also has responsibility for providing residential accommodation for disabled people and its powers in this area stem from section 12 of the Health Services and Public Health Act 1968 and section 2 of the National Health Service Reorganisation Act 1973. These powers enable the NHS to provide residential accommodation for physically handicapped people in units which are usually YDUs, but the medical emphasis is often retained, even in the title when they are called 'young chronic sick units'.

While the first of these units was opened in 1968, the building programme for new units was accelerated after the passage of the Chronically Sick and Disabled Persons Act 1970, for section 17 requires that:

In any hospital a person who is suffering from a condition of chronic illness or disability is not cared for in the hospital as an in-patient in any part of the hospital which is normally used wholly or mainly for the care of elderly persons, unless he is himself an elderly person.

According to a recent national survey (Bloomfield, 1976) there were forty-one operational YDUs in Britain in 1975 in comparison with thirty purpose-built local authority homes (Goldsmith, 1976). Both social services and health authorities had plans for a considerable number of additional units but economic circumstances and consumer resistance have slowed down building programmes.

Thus there are three main agencies providing residential accommodation for disabled people: social services, the health service and the Cheshire Foundation. There is no clear distinction between them, and while the majority of Cheshire homes are registered as disabled persons' homes under section 37 of the National Assistance Act 1948, some are registered as nursing homes under section 187 of the Public Health Act 1936 as amended by section 41 of the National Health Service Reorganisation Act 1973. In practice those establishments registered as nursing homes are able to take hospital-sponsored residents, usually the arrangement being that a certain number of beds in the home are contracted to the health authority and available to its 'patients'.

The complexities of these legal arrangements do not in practice mean that there is a clear division of function between the three kinds of homes, for, as Goldsmith points out:

> There is no clear demarcation line at which a handicapped person becomes a hospital rather than a local authority responsibility and no firm guidelines are set down by the Department of Health . . . There is thus no clear distinction between hospital sponsored residents and local authority residents, demonstrated by the Cheshire Homes which cater for both categories of residents (where residents commonly do not know who is on which side).

> (Goldsmith, 1976, p. 76)

However, Goldsmith goes on to suggest that administrative procedures relating to these legislative requirements do allow the voluntary sector and local authorities to reject people who are in need of 'continuous nursing care' and therefore that the hospital units often become the last refuge. He also points out that voluntary homes can be more selective than local authority ones and cites evidence from Miller and Gwynne (1971), who found a higher instance of emotional disorders in local authority homes.

Residential accommodation for disabled people: a provision under attack

Since the publication of *Asylums* (Goffman, 1961) a considerable amount of work on the effects of institutionalisation has been done. 'Total institutions', as Goffman called them, are characterised by a loss of privacy, a lack of freedom of choice, and the individual within them misses the opportunity to make meaningful personal relationships. The institution provides a highly structured routine where the lives of the individual residents are regulated by management and all tend to be treated alike. This gives rise to what has been identified as institutional neurosis:

> a disease characterised by apathy, lack of intitiative, loss of interest more marked in things and events not immediately personal or present, submissiveness, and sometimes no expression of feelings or resentment at harsh or unfair orders. There is also a lack of interest in the future and an apparent inability to make practical plans for it, a deterioration in personal habits, toilet and standards generally, a loss of individuality, and a resigned acceptance that things will go on as they are – unchangingly, inevitably and indefinitely.

(Barton, 1959)

Such studies as are specifically concerned with institutions for disabled people have tended to see the effects of institutionalisation on the residents in less dramatic terms than Goffman. The 'warehousing' model of residential care described by Miller and Gwynne (1971) in *A Life Apart*, and which they call the conventional approach to residential care, approximates to Goffman's total institution in its requirement that the inmate remain dependent and depersonalised and subjugated to the task of the institution. The authors were 'captured by the plight of intelligent cripples . . . who were forced to lead stunted lives in institutions that do not provide opportunities for their development'. But they do not portray the residents they met in the negative terms used by Barton, for instance; two possible differences are that schizophrenic patients studied by Barton are particularly vulnerable to institutionalisation and that the psychiatric hospital is more of a 'closed' community than the residential home for disabled people. In another study of a home for the disabled, Musgrove

(1977) describes a visit to a Cheshire home, which he saw as fitting Goffman's picture of a total institution only in a very superficial way, as the residents were not completely regimented, and he was struck, contrary to his expectation, by the extent to which they had managed to maintain their sense of identity.

However, in a view from the inside (as opposed to Musgrove's outsider view), Battye, who experienced life as a resident in both the chronic ward of a long-stay hospital and a Cheshire home, saw the difference between the two, in spite of the more favourable life-style of the latter, as one only of degree, not of kind:

> Unless he fights a constant battle to retain his intellectual integrity and sense of purpose, as the years go by he will gradually feel the atmosphere of the place closing in on him as it did in the chronic ward . . . in spite of efforts to arouse or retain his interest in life he will feel boredom and apathy creeping over him like a slow paralysis eroding his will, dulling his critical wits, dousing his spirit, killing his independence . . . In a subtler, more civilised way than in the chronic ward, he will have become institutionalised.

> (Battye, 1966, p. 14)

Miller and Gwynne (1971) in their study of local authority and voluntary homes draw the distinction between 'warehousing' and 'horticultural' models of residential care. The warehousing model expresses the humanitarian or medical value that the prolongation of life is a good thing but the question concerning the purpose of the life that is prolonged is never asked. The emphasis is on medical care and the minimisation of risk — the main aim is to keep the gap between social death (the point when the disabled person enters the institution) and physical death as long as possible. Alternatively the horticultural model emphasises the uniqueness of each inmate, the importance of individual responsibility, and the potential to realise unfulfilled ambitions and capacities.

The horticultural model itself may give rise to problems, and Miller and Gwynne (1971) themselves point to some of their concerns over the overvaluing of independence, the denial of disability and the distortion of staff—resident relations where the real facts of the situation are ignored or distorted. Hunt (1981), himself disabled, takes them to task over their failure to give whole-hearted endorsement to the horticultural model: 'The liberal growth approach, whatever criticisms may be made of some of its theories and assumptions, represents a genuine advance towards securing the rights and freedoms of a civilised life for many handicapped people.' There have been few attempts to implement completely the horticultural model and no evaluations of its effectiveness. However, impressionistic evidence from one residential home (Dartington *et al.*, 1981) which operates broadly within this model endorses Hunt's statement.

It is not just voluntary and local authority homes which have come in for such criticism but YDUs also. Bloomfield in her national survey argues:

> While it cannot be denied that many of the inmates of Younger Chronic Sick Units require extensive help with personal care, it is refuted that this help can only be provided in a hospital setting. By focusing on this one aspect of the inmates' requirements, the Younger Chronic Sick Unit systematically robs the individual of the opportunity for achieving satisfaction and purpose in the life remaining to him. The unavoidable emphasis on his physical dependence on authoritative personnel frequently leads all but the strongest individuals to an accepting, apathetic state with little interest in life and even less initiative.
>
> (Bloomfield, 1976)

When the health authority in Rochdale attempted to build a YDU, it met with such resistance that it had to abandon their plans (Finlay, 1978), and the same happened in Surrey (North Surrey CHC, 1978). Internal and external criticisms of the residential care sector coupled with consumer resistance have in recent years forced providers to look to possible alternatives. Many criticisms of residential care implicitly draw upon the social model of disability in that they see institutional regimes as adding to rather than alleviating many of the problems that disabled individuals face.

Alternative models of residential care

The disabled village

This is based on the village settlement at Het Dorp in Holland where around 400 severely disabled people are accommodated in one colony. Approximately 80 per cent of the residents are single but there are a number of married couples where both parties are severely handicapped. Each resident has a self-contained flat, and services such as meals and staff care are provided on site.

The argument in favour of this sort of development is that it does allow severely handicapped residents to take control of their own lives. However, the village has not successfully integrated into the wider community and it has become a 'cripples' colony' with little mixing of disabled and non-disabled people. There are a couple of similar settlements in Britain, most notably the Thistle Foundation Village in Edinburgh and the Papworth Settlement in Cambridgeshire.

Collective houses

A number of these have sprung up in Denmark whereby the tenancies of blocks of flats are allocated on the approximate ration of one disabled person to three able-bodied ones. Consumer services such as restaurants are contained within the blocks and the aim was to move away from institutions and colonies. Unfortunately, this ratio has tended to be rather high and internal social divisions between the disabled and the able-bodied have occurred. Additionally the outside world has continued to regard those houses as institutions for the disabled.

While collective houses have not developed on a large scale

outside Denmark, there have been a few isolated experiments
in Britain where severely disabled people have lived in flats
where other able-bodied tenants provided physical assistance
in exchange for lower rents. Probably the most successful
example of this kind of development, though on a smaller
scale than the Danish collective houses, is the Grove Road
scheme (Davis, 1981). Not only did it provide an appropriate
housing environment, but the disabled people were able to
manage with less than one-third of the direct physical assistance that they had needed while in residential care, and they
were also able to prove wrong all of the professional assessments which had labelled them 'too disabled to live in the
community'.

Fokus housing

This has developed in Sweden and has been an attempt to
integrate severely handicapped people into ordinary housing
schemes. Supportive services are provided and there are a
range of communal facilities available. It is estimated that
there are now over 2,000 severely disabled people living in
this type of accommodation in Sweden.

While these schemes have moved a long way towards
integration of handicapped people, it has been suggested that
some of the trappings of institutionalisation remain and that
not all of the handicapped tenants become part of the
community.

In Britain many housing authorities now attempt to integrate housing for disabled people into their new schemes.
However, such disabled people rely on community medical
and nursing service for support and these are often too remote
or inflexible to allow severely handicapped people to live in
the community without a great deal of family support.

Independent living units

This started as a number of isolated experiments in the USA
and has now developed into a movement (De Jong, 1981).
What has happened is that small groups of severely handicapped people have banded together for physical, economic

and emotional reasons, rented or taken over buildings and thereby managed to live independently. By pooling all resources they have managed to obtain suitable property, found the courage to move from institutions and reasserted control over their own lives in such areas as the hiring and firing of their own care staff. These units approximate to normal living and appear to provide for meaningful integration into the community. There are up to 1983 no such experiments in Britain, though there do exist plans to establish such a centre in Hampshire.

British housing association schemes

These are usually assemblies of between twelve and twenty-five flats grouped together to form a 'mini-colony', often with a warden or caretaker to oversee the residents. These are usually built in an urban setting and close to the main services and are purpose-designed to maximise independent living.

There are a number of examples of this type of provision including Friendship House at Poole, built by the Raglan Housing Association, and Princes Crescent, Finsbury Park, built by the John Grooms Housing Association. Usually these schemes require that the tenants can cope independently, but in theory there is no reason why supportive care staff could not be provided either externally through a Crossroads care-attendant scheme or internally by making architectural provision for staff to live in. It is interesting to note that some of the most important voluntary organisations in the residential care sector have set up their own housing associations to provide suitable accommodation in the community — notably the Spastics Society, John Grooms and more recently the Cheshire Foundation. The most recent development is that Shelter, the housing charity, is planning to develop a number of similar projects throughout the country in conjunction with the newly formed British Council of Organisations of Disabled People.

While many of these schemes may remove the worst effects of institutionalisation, it has been suggested that they do not truly integrate disabled people into the community, but rather provide a more sympathetic, though still isolated, physical environment. Thus they only go some way towards removing the disabling effects of institutionalisation.

Social work, the social model and residential care

The social model suggests that disability is imposed upon impaired individuals as a consequence of the way society is organised. There can be little doubt that residential care in most cases does indeed further disable impaired individuals, and from this viewpoint residential care offers an unacceptable form of provision, at least as it is presently organised.

It is easy to see how by working within the individual model of disability those involved in planning and providing services for people with disabilities are led to see residential provision as a suitable option when an impaired individual is no longer able to continue living as previously, either as a consequence of family break up, community support and/or increasing impairment. The question for those charged with responsibility for providing a service from within the individual model then automatically becomes: what does the individual need? The answer logically is food, clothing, shelter and personal assistance, and when individual needs are aggregated it seems not unreasonable to meet these needs through the provision of residential accommodation for a number of individuals.

The question service providers should ask from within the social model, however, is a different one, and becomes: in what ways does the physical and social environment prevent this impaired individual from remaining in the community and continuing to live a normal life? This obviously produces a different answer along the lines of the need for suitable and adequate housing, a reasonable income to ensure access to food, clothing and personal assistance, the provision of community support, and so on.

The first social work task, then, is to ensure that those who are at risk of being forced to go into residential care are given the option of remaining in the community with adequate support. Of course, some may wish to go into residential care, and this should be a real choice available, but impaired people should not be forced into becoming further disabled because residential care is the only option available. The social services department and the social worker must aim to provide a range of options which maximises choice, and some of the alternatives just discussed should be considered instead of building yet more homes along traditional lines.

Having said that, there are many people already in residential care and social workers may have a role to play in working with them. Thus 'physically or mentally handicapped people in residential care may not only require good physical care, but they may also need help to overcome the effects their respective disabilities may have upon their personal and social lives and relationships' (Payne, 1978, p. 60).

These disabilities, following the social model, are a consequence of the institutionalisation of people and not a result of their impairments, and consequently solutions may involve some or all of the following:

1. The demedicalisation of residential care with a move away from matrons, doctors, nursing staff and uniforms, and in particular with regard to YDUs the separation of them from hospitals.
2. Increasing the privacy and autonomy of individual residents by providing more single rooms so that all residents can have access to privacy. Residents should be allowed to lock their own doors, provide their own furniture and live in the style they choose, including making their own decisions, about when to go to bed, get up and what meals to eat and where to eat them.
3. Developing more constructive activities including gainful employment and ordinary living activities such as cooking, washing, ironing and cleaning.
4. Allowing more access to the outside world. Although the mobility allowance has gone some way towards making this easier, there are obvious difficulties for those homes deep in the countryside. Furthermore, residents in YDUs may not be allowed out unaccompanied due to NHS regulations.
5. Bringing the outside world in, though this should only be done at the behest of the residents, for there is nothing

more degrading and depersonalising than conducted tours by local dignitaries of what, after all, are people's homes. Everyone, disabled or not, surely has the right to decide who can enter their own homes and people in residential care must be accorded that same basic right.

These suggestions offer achievable ways of improving the lives of those currently in residential care. And of course they do not preclude the provision of counselling services as well, for some residents may indeed wish, and need, to have access to that kind of therapeutic relationship. However, it would be an unfortunate mistake to attempt to provide personal counselling for all residents without questioning the need for improvements within the institution itself.

Another social work task might therefore be to protect vulnerable people from the disabling consequences of their environments. Shearer indicts social workers for failing so to do with regard to disabled children on the 'special care' wards of hospitals:

> The social workers who might have been expected to show concern for the appalling standards of child-care on the wards commonly saw this as none of their concern: one had nothing to do with them because 'these children will never be discharged'.
>
> (Shearer, 1981a, p. 102)

There is obviously a dilemma for social workers who desperately need a residential place for clients but are less than happy with what is available. While there are no easy answers, it is worth remembering that local authorities pay fees for such accommodation, and the social worker as representative of the authority is entitled to have a say.

The issue of payments is one way in which the whole system of residential care disables not just impaired residents but social workers also. Local authorities, private and voluntary homes each charge for their beds, and these charges range from £60–300 a week, whereas beds in YDUs or private and voluntary homes registered under the Public Health Act 1936 rather than the National Assistance Act 1948 are provided free as they are regarded as NHS beds. This further disables residents in that they have their incomes assessed in part III homes and are effectively constrained from working, for they would be forced to give up almost all that they earned. While in theory no such charges apply to those in NHS beds, if you are in hospital, you are sick and therefore cannot work.

Social workers are disabled in trying to make the best of this system for their clients. As has already been suggested, there is no evidence that the different sectors cater for different clientele and therefore it is usually a matter of what is available at any particular time. Thus it may be a matter of chance whether clients may have to give up their financial independence depending on whether they are offered a part III or a NHS bed. The artificial divisions that financial charges impose prevent a co-ordinated and effective use of residential accommodation. Indeed, the social worker, if able to spend less time on financial assessments and form-filling, might have time to ensure that the kind of accommodation offered was commensurate with the needs of the client.

There is one further issue to consider and that concerns the additional functions of residential care, which does not exist solely to meet the needs of residents. Goffman drew attention to this when he wrote:

> If all the institutions in a given region were emptied and closed down today, tomorrow parents, relatives, police, judges, doctors and social workers would raise a clamour for new ones: and these the true clients of the institution would demand new institutions to satisfy their needs.

> (Goffman, 1961, p. 334)

In the last chapter it was suggested that physical impairment disables other family members, particularly spouses or daughters, and residential care is increasingly being used on a short-term basis in order to give carers a break. In many cases the disabled person is perfectly prepared to go into care on a short-term basis, but some refuse and this may place the social worker in a dilemma: Who should be regarded as the client?

Whose needs should take precedence? If more community support were available, it might be possible to provide the carer with a break without resort to residential care; if residential care were better, people might enter into it more willingly. Ultimately, however, the social worker may be faced with attempts to reconcile conflicting interests, and such work will inevitably require a long-term casework approach with the whole family if the ultimate outcome of permanent residential care and complete family break up is to be avoided.

Day-care facilities

One important resource available to the social worker and the disabled person which may prevent family break up and admittance to residential care is the day centre. By going to a day centre on a regular basis, the stresses and strains can be alleviated in the carer and the disabled person can also receive a wider range of experiences than would otherwise be available. However, as with residential care, there are a number of criticisms that can be levelled at day care which call into question the extent of its usefulness.

One criticism is that day centres are themselves often segregative, and while most of the buildings may be located in urban settings their use is often restricted to the 'client group'. Many centres organise their activities around the idea of work, though those participating are paid a maximum of only £4 a week. This has led some critics to state that

> To expect disabled people to do boring work and to do it for a pittance does seem to smack of exploitation . . . We consider that thirty hours a week packing greasy gaskets for a mere £2 or so is the modern equivalent of oakum-picking, with some of the same thinking behind it.
>
> (Tuckey and Tuckey, 1981, p. 12)

Defenders of such activities point to two things in its favour: they suggest that for many users 'proper work', even for a pittance, is more rewarding than middle-class activities like basket-making, painting and craft work; they further argue that even if they wanted to pay more money this is impossible because social security regulations will not allow it and also many disabled people do not do enough work to 'earn' the money.

The real criticism of centres based upon work is that the need to fulfil contracts and meet target dates often dominates the life of centres and prevents sufficient attention being given to other needs and activities. Furthermore, such contracts are usually negotiated by centre managers or other departmental staff and not by the disabled clientele themselves. This leads to another criticism of centres, even those organised around the idea of 'care': that is, that they are essentially paternalistic, and in the majority of cases disabled people are the passive recipients of day-care services. In short, impaired people are often further disabled by the regimes of the day centres available to them.

Another important criticism of day centres concerns the mixing of age ranges and client groups. A national survey highlighted the first of these problems:

> These twenty-five centres deal with users who are young, middle-aged and old but there are a preponderance of people who . . . are at the ageing end of the scale. A quarter of the users interviewed in social service centres were under 40, but nearly half were older people aged 60 or more. This means that some centres labelled as venues for the physically handicapped could equally be classified as centres for the elderly.
>
> (Carter, 1981, p. 64)

With regard to working alongside other client groups Tuckey and Tuckey point out:

> While it may be that helping or working alongside the mentally ill, the mentally handicapped or the socially inadequate would be beneficial to some disabled people, it is not likely that the majority of disabled people, any more than the majority of non-disabled people, would choose to spend their time in this way even if paid to do

so. Social Services departments should bear in mind that not everyone shares the preoccupations of social workers.

(Tuckey and Tuckey, 1981, p. 48)

Day care, then, like residential care, can be criticised on a number of grounds and this obviously poses a dilemma for the social worker wishing to use it as a resource. Should people be referred to a centre where the regime is seen as being unacceptable or should the need of the carer for a break be regarded as paramount? Of course, neither extreme position needs to be taken and it is perfectly possible to place someone in a centre while pressing for changes in the organisation and functioning of the centre at the same time. Tuckey and Tuckey (1981) provide a descriptive account of the kind of day centre that is more appropriate to the needs of disabled people, and indeed compatible with the social model of disability, a centre whose title (*An Ordinary Place*) encapsulates its basic philosophy. Of course, the chances of achieving organisational change are limited where there is poor co-ordination between the social services department and the day centre, as in one extreme case where the centre manager will not allow divisional staff into the centre.

Residential and day care are two of the resources available to people living with disabilities and to social workers who may be involved with them. However, there are two basic questions which hang over both kinds of resource, from the point of view of both providers and users: How appropriate are such resources? What can be done to improve them. It is hoped that this chapter has provided a suitable background against which to debate these questions, if not to answer them satisfactorily.

6

The Legal and Social Context of Disability

Living within a family or in residential accommodation can be disabling for impaired people. In the wider context all impaired people are disabled to a greater or lesser degree by the society in which they live. The social model of disability suggests that impaired people in Britain may face educational disability, employment disability and economic disability, and it is perhaps somewhat ironic that some of the legal measures taken to combat such disadvantages actually further contribute to the disabling process. This chapter will focus upon some aspects of this relationship between disabled people and society and consider some of the possible intervention strategies for social workers. To begin with the discussion needs to be placed in the context of legislation relating to disability.

The legal rights of disabled people

While it is indeed possible to trace state involvement and concern with the physically disabled back to 1601 and beyond, there is little need to go back further than the 1940s, when the foundations of the welfare state were laid. Prior to this, statutory provision for disabled people had been made on a piecemeal or *ad hoc* basis and often only related to specific types of disability or the way in which disabilities had been caused. While this specificity has not been completely eradicated, state provision is now geared towards disabled people as a single group.

The first Act of Parliament to treat disabled people as one single category of persons was the Disabled Persons (Employment) Act 1944. Not only did this attempt to ensure that employers employed a certain number of disabled workers but it also made provision for the assessment of employment potential, the establishment of rehabilitation centres and the provision of vocational training courses and maintenance grants for those selected to attend them. Subsequently the National Health Service Act 1946, while providing for the acute medical needs of disabled people, also made it possible for local authority health departments to provide any medical equipment or aids necessary to keep people in their own homes. The National Assistance Act 1948 made some provision for meeting the financial needs of disabled people and in addition imposed a duty on local authorities to provide residential accommodation and services for 'persons who are substantially and permanently handicapped by illness, injury or congenital deformity'. In addition the Education Act 1944 stated that every child should receive education suitable for his age, ability and aptitude and to provide special educational treatment for those thought to need it.

These Acts form the cornerstone of statutory provision for disabled people and subsequent legislation has merely altered, modified or extended existing provision. The current situation regarding education and employment will be discussed separately, but to begin with consideration needs to be given to perhaps the most important and certainly the most publicised piece of legislation of all, the Chronically Sick and Disabled Persons Act 1970. This sought to give disabled people the right to live in the community, by providing appropriate support services. The Act imposes two duties on local authorities:

(a) the duty to inform themselves of the number and needs of handicapped persons in their areas
(b) the duty to publicise available services

Further, section 2 lists various services which should be provided for those whose needs have been assessed, and these may include:

(a) practical assistance in the home
(b) recreational facilities both in the home and outside
(c) travel facilities, either free or subsidised
(d) social work support to families
(e) adaptations to the home and special equipment including telephones
(f) holiday arrangements
(g) meals

The Act is regarded by some (Topliss and Gould, 1981) as nothing less than 'a charter for the disabled', its very presence constituting nothing less than public acknowledgement of the social rights of disabled people. However, the evidence for this is somewhat tenuous, and Topliss and Gould argue that

> Society may in fact have expended too little in the way of resources and effort to adjust the environment, as much as many would wish, to meet the needs of disabled people, but the acceptance of an obligation to move in this direction has never been challenged since the passing of the Act.
>
> (Topliss and Gould, 1981, p. 142)

It is further claimed that the passage of the Act and its subsequent presence have also increased public awareness of disability and changed attitudes towards disabled people. Finally, it is often claimed that the Act at last laid down a statutory framework for services to which disabled people were entitled.

There are a number of criticisms that can be levelled at this evaluation of the Act. To begin with, one commentator has noted that 'In the main, Section 2 of the Chronically Sick and Disabled Persons Act . . . is only Section 29 of the National Assistance Act 1948 writ large' (Keeble, 1979, p. 40).

It has also been claimed that the Act was a watershed in the lives of disabled people, and undoubtedly there has been a very real improvement in services for handicapped people in the last decade. However, criticism has been noted of the Act in that it 'appears to make a lot of highly satisfactory promises but careful analysis of Section 2 reveals that nothing must of necessity be provided outright, let alone free' (Keeble, 1979, p. 41).

There has certainly been concern expressed that the Act promises more than it actually delivers and a recent national survey concluded: 'The CSDP surveys found handicapped people requiring and wanting help who were not in regular contact with any of the professional caring services and some who, although in contact with one service, needed help from another' (Knight and Warren, 1978, p. 70). The economic crisis and subsequent cutbacks have exacerbated these problems and some authorities have withdrawn services previously provided.

Another criticism often made (Shearer, 1981b; Knight and Warren, 1978) is that services are often provided on the basis of locality rather than on need. There is considerable variability between local authorities about what services they provide and, unfortunately, it is still true that the best professional advice for some disabled people is to 'move'!

A more serious criticism stems from the RADAR project undertaken by fifteen major disability organisations which is attempting to clarify the law regarding this particular piece of legislation. Despite some limited success in individual cases it is clear from the published report (Cook and Mitchell, 1982) that, given the current economic climate and the often uneasy relationship between central and local government, the Act is neither implementable nor enforceable.

Finally, Shearer (1981b) is not just critical of the Act's failure to meet need and provide services, but also of its underlying philosophy, which, she suggests, takes away from disabled people the crucial element of choice:

> The offer of a holiday at a time and in a place that suits the social service worker or local authority, rather than cash in hand to spend according to individual preference, sits oddly with the rhetoric which asserts that people with disabilities should have greater access to the range of social choices that many of the rest of society take for granted. The substitution of kind for cash sits no less uneasily with aspirations to enhance the self-determination and dignity of people with disabilities, in a society where status and respect has so much to do with purchasing power. The potential public outcry against a paternalistic

state which attempted to deliver, say, child benefit in the form of nappies, creams and baby foods, does not take much imagining.

(Shearer, 1981b, pp. 82—3)

She thus suggests that the Act's underlying philosophy is a step in the wrong direction and that what disabled people in fact need is more cash and strong anti-discrimination legislation to ensure that they can buy the kinds of services they need.

More will be said of anti-discrimination later in the chapter, but it is worth remembering that, whatever its defects, the Chronically Sick and Disabled Persons Act provides the main legal framework within which social workers, particularly those employed in social services departments, have to work. A crucial problem for social workers (and OTs and other professionals) is that very often they know there are not the resources available to meet the needs they encounter, and yet to acknowledge these needs may well place a legal obligation upon their employer to meet such needs. The problem then centres on differences between administrative and professional definitions of need, and unfortunately most professionals have received little assistance from their own associations in advancing their own professional definitions. It is scarcely credible to imagine doctors refusing to diagnose illnesses because there are not sufficient resources available to treat all those so diagnosed, and other professionals should learn from this self-confidence.

There are a number of informal solutions to this dilemma: social workers may suggest that clients take their complaints to the politicians and have even been known to draft letters themselves, and others have contacted the RADAR project anonymously. However, while such tactics may resolve discrepancies between need and provision in individual cases, they do not tackle wider issues concerning conflicts between administrative and professional definitions of need, nor do they make the Act ultimately more implementable or enforceable. To be a client (or indeed a social worker) in a service where expectations and needs far outweigh available resources can be a disabling experience in itself. None the less one cannot help feeling that more disabled people would get the services to which they are entitled if professionals were to act as advocates of that need rather than rationing agents of their employers.

Education

The Education Act 1944 laid a duty on local authorities to have regard 'to the need for securing that provision is made for pupils who suffer from any disability of the mind and body by providing, either in special schools or otherwise, special educational treatment'. It also obliged the authorities to ascertain the numbers of children in their areas who required special educational treatment. The Act was important for handicapped children and their families in that it gave them legal rights to education, but unfortunately it left it to the authorities and to professionals to determine exactly what kind of education was appropriate.

Even more unfortunately, responsible authorities have chosen to make provision for the special needs of disabled children in segregated establishments of one kind or another. Despite mounting criticism of special education in recent years, both on the grounds of its failure to provide an adequate or comparable education to that provided in ordinary schools, and the social implications of segregating large numbers of children from their peers, both the numbers and percentage of the school population in special schools has grown steadily, as Table 6.1 clearly shows.

In recognition of the growing controversies surrounding the educational needs of disabled children, the government set up a Committee of Enquiry which produced the Warnock Report in 1978. The Report made numerous recommendations, including replacing the original categories of handicapped children with the broader concept of 'special educational needs' and the government issued a White Paper in 1980 called *Special Needs in Education* which broadly endorsed the proposals of the Warnock Report. While Warnock, the White Paper and the subsequent legislation, the Education

Table 6.1 *Numbers and percentage of school population in special schools*

Year	Numbers	Percentage
1950	47,000	0.75
1955	58,000	0.81
1960	66,000	0.86
1965	74,000	0.96
1970	87,000	1.01
1975	132,000	1.37
1977	135,000	1.39

Source: Booth (1981, p. 293).

Act 1981, favoured the idea of integration, it made no extra resources available to facilitate such a move. The 1981 Act leaves the legal rights of parents and their handicapped children unchanged and it is still the local authority which decides what educational provision is appropriate.

There are important implications in this continued commitment to special schools, for, as Tomlinson has shown, this is not based solely on the humanitarian ideal of providing what is best for handicapped children, but also that 'provision developed to cater for the needs of ordinary schools, the interests of the wider industrial society and the specific interests of professionals' (Tomlinson, 1982, p. 57).

It could be argued that all this is of little relevance to social work. However, it is clear that more and more parents are beginning to demand that their children be educated in ordinary schools, and in order to achieve those demands against the opposition of vested interests, talked about by Tomlinson, then parents will need help. They will perhaps need advocates to intercede on their behalf and argue that it is not in the best interests of the child, either educationally or socially, that he or she be deprived of family life and links with peers and community for substantial periods during the formative years. Social workers may be ideally placed by virtue of regular contact since the birth of the disabled child to help families negotiate with the education authorities, though at present it seems that they are reluctant to take on this advocacy role and to challenge decisions made by their local authority colleagues.

What is clear is that in the future, with or without help, increasing numbers of parents will demand the social rights to an ordinary education for their children, for it is clear that for many impaired children segregated education adds educational and social disability to existing disadvantages.

Employment

The Disabled Persons (Employment) Act 1944 laid a framework for the provision of a variety of employment rehabilitation and resettlement services. It also gave disabled people legal rights to employment, in that it placed an obligation on all employers employing more than twenty workers to employ a quota of 3 per cent of the work-force who were registered as disabled. It is not an offence for employers to be below their quota but if they are an exemption permit is needed before any vacancies can be filled with non-disabled workers. These permits should only be issued if there is no suitable disabled person available, but in practice employers are issued with bulk permits every six months with very little scrutiny of their employment practices.

Despite these legal rights it remains true that disabled workers are more likely to be unemployed than their able-bodied counterparts. Grover and Gladstone summarise the situation as follows:

> In 1965 the general unemployment rate was well below 2 per cent but among registered disabled people, over 7 per cent. Until the mid-1970s this group was never less than three times more likely to be unemployed. Over the last five years the gap has narrowed considerably, not because unemployment among disabled people has abated but because of a massive rise in general unemployment. Today the general rate is something over 12 per cent while among registered disabled people it is nearly 16 per cent. If the trend continues, disabled workers, though worse off than they were, will soon obtain equality of opportunity.

. . . In fact, what seems to be happening is that employers are relatively less willing to dismiss disabled workers already on their books. But they are also becoming less willing to take on *new* disabled workers. In 1979/80 MSC's Disablement Resettlement Officers were able to place 60,000 disabled people in open employment but in 1980/81 only 39,500 — a fall of 34 per cent. If *this* trend continues, unemployment among disabled people will reach unprecedented levels.

(Grover and Gladstone, 1982, p. 1)

In addition there has been widespread evasion of their duties by employers; in 1980 only 35 per cent of firms complied with their quota obligations. Despite this widespread evasion, there have only been ten prosecutions since the Act became law in 1944. There are different views as to why this should be so, the Manpower Services Commission arguing that the Act is unenforceable and disabled people and their organisations suggesting that the MSC prefers persuasion and lacks the will to attempt enforcement. An American observer, Professor Stubbins, captures the essentials of this debate:

The majority of personnel in the resettlement service favored repeal of its mandatory features. With even greater unanimity, the disabled and their organizations favored retention. This difference in viewpoint might suggest the great divide between career civil servants concerned with employment rehabilitation and those who experience disability directly. Personally, I thought it remarkable that ESD [Employment Services Division] persisted in fomenting another review of the quota scheme in 1979–80 despite the fact that there was plenty of evidence that the rehabilitation community itself believed its continuation was essential. There was a suggestion that officials consistently attributed more importance to the views of employers and the trades unions than to the broad constituency of the disabled. This is undoubtedly proper when considering matters relating to the provision of general employment and training services. However, it was surprising to find that, where specialist services were concerned, more weight was not given to the representatives of potential clients, the disabled themselves.

(in Brechin *et al.*, 1981, p. 201)

The review referred to was published by the MSC in 1981 and suggests the replacement of the quota system with a statutory code of practice, but whether the government will accept its recommendations and change the current legal position remains uncertain.

What is certain, as far as social work intervention is concerned, is that often the major problem that many disabled people face is that of unemployment, and again the question arises as to whether it is part of the social work task to attempt to alleviate such problems. Interestingly social workers have tended to be more critical of disablement resettlement officers (DROs) than they have of other professionals working in the area of special education, but have not taken their task much beyond criticism. This is perhaps unfortunate, for if unemployment is assessed as the major problem, more than criticism may be needed. Most local authorities themselves will be below quota and it is therefore perfectly possible for social workers to attempt to get disabled people employed in their own departments and agencies, rather than simply seeing employment as the responsibility of the DRO. In addition there are many people in day and residential care who are capable of carrying out the administrative and organisational tasks connected with the day-to-day running of such places. For example, it hardly seems professionally justifiable or cost effective for a local day centre to use a retired army major who is visually handicapped to pack knife blades while employing someone who is able-bodied to perform clerical and administrative duties connected with the particular day centre concerned. Thus social workers who have unemployed disabled clients should be prepared to see finding a job as part of their task and they should be much more imaginative and practical about how they go about it, ensuring that their own employers meet their obligations as well as criticising others who fail to do so. This is one way that social workers might contribute to the task of reducing employment disability among their clients.

Welfare rights

The term 'welfare rights' can be interpreted in two ways: in its broadest sense it can mean the rights of the individual to all of the services provided by the welfare state; in its narrower sense it may mean the social security benefit entitlements that individuals may have. While recognising the broad use of the term, which might encompass legal and social rights as well, in this section the term will be confined to its usage in reference to the financial benefits and entitlements of disabled people.

Simkins and Tickner (1978), in their study of the financial benefit systems for disabled people, found that no less than fifty-five separate welfare benefits were available to disabled people. Despite this seemingly generous provision, numerous studies have shown the clear connection between poverty and disability. For example, Townsend showed that half of the appreciably or severely disabled people in the United Kingdom were living in poverty, compared with only one-fifth of able-bodied people, and he further showed that even where disabled people were in work they were poorer than their able-bodied counterparts. He concludes:

> Not only do disabled people have lower social status. They also have lower incomes and fewer assets. Moreover, they tend to be poorer even when their social status is the same as the non-disabled . . . With increasing incapacity, proportionately more people lived in households with incomes below, or only marginally above that standard. Fewer lived in households with relatively high incomes.
>
> (Townsend, 1979, p. 711)

There are a number of reasons that have been suggested for the persistence of chronic poverty among disabled people. It

is sometimes argued that the level of benefits is set at too low
a level, and certainly evidence produced by the Royal Commission on the Distribution of Income and Wealth which
reported in 1978 indicates that despite a proliferation of
benefits throughout the 1970s the relative position of disabled
people as a group has not changed significantly. Another
reason concerns the 'take-up' of various benefits, for some
people may not know of their existence, while others may
feel that application (and certainly appeal) is a stigmatising
business and refuse to claim. A final reason concerns the
complexity of the system, with its overlapping benefits,
different eligibility criteria and other administrative problems,
that often make claiming a nightmare. The difficulties of the
'welfare-benefits jungle' are well captured by Simkins and
Tickner:

> To illustrate the tangle of criteria needed to make the
> present system work, let us consider a person with one
> or both legs amputated. If he is seeking a payment under
> War Pensions or Industrial Injury schemes, he must first
> establish where and how the damage was caused, and
> then the size of the payment made to the amputee would
> depend on a schedule, in 10 per cent steps, in effect
> needing a reply to the question: 'how much of the limb/
> limbs have you lost?'
>
> For the Mobility Allowance the question would be
> 'are you unable or virtually unable to walk, and likely to
> remain so?' — the applicant who can walk a relatively
> short distance with the help of artificial limbs may not
> get the allowance even if he has no feet.
>
> If an Attendance Allowance were being sought, the
> question is 'how much help do you have to have?'
>
> For the contributory benefits the approach is 'never
> mind the leg, how about your payments record?'
>
> For Supplementary Benefits, or to find out how
> much a home help would cost (if one is available), the
> question is 'how poor are you?' and for some local
> authority benefits, 'how isolated are you from relatives
> whom we might expect to help you?'
>
> For some local authority benefits the key question

may well be 'where do you live?' For a few people who lived in the wrong spot at the time of local government boundary reorganisation, entitlement vanished overnight without the applicant moving from his bed.

And of course if the amputee is a 'housewife', the authorities are not interested in her leg, only in the answer to: 'what kind of contribution record or income does your husband have?' And for the single woman: 'are you cohabiting with a man to whom you are not married?' [The new phrase is 'living with a man who is not your husband'.]

(Simkins and Tickner, 1978, pp. 51–2)

Given that these criticisms are valid, there seem to be three fairly simple solutions to the problems of poverty and disability: raise the level of benefits; make them available as a right and reduce the number of eligibility tests; and finally, simplify the system. However, these are not realistic possibilities in the short term, and for the social worker, who has a disabled client whose poverty is current, immediate action is necessary.

The first approach is to make sure that the client is receiving all the entitled benefits, and in order to do that the social worker may need to resort to additional help — otherwise the myths that some professionals hold like 'you can't get attendance allowance if you work', or 'you can't get mobility allowance if you can walk', will continue to abound. The first place to start is with the *Disability Rights Handbook*, which is produced every year by the Disability Alliance with the Spastics Society and is the simplest yet most accurate and comprehensive guide to welfare benefits and it is a guide that both social workers and their disabled clients can use. If more expert advice is needed then the Disablement Income Group (DIG), the Disability Alliance or other local organisations like Disablement Information and Advice Line (DIAL) may be able to help, not just with information but also possibly with representation at appeals or tribunals. In short, in order to minimise poverty and reduce economic disability, it is important that disabled people receive all the benefits to which they are entitled.

A second approach is to set up a disability rights project where a number of disabled people in a particular area or day centre are assessed by welfare rights experts to see whether they are getting all that they are entitled to. The most spectacularly successful such project was undertaken in Strathclyde (Casserly and Clark, 1978), where seventy-two disabled people attending a day centre were assessed as to their entitlements. Only six were receiving their full entitlement and a further fifty had their benefits increased, on average by £6.10 a week (1977 figures) and overall the group's income was increased by over £15,000 per annum. Other similar projects in Harlow, Leeds and North Yorkshire have also substantially increased benefits for disabled people and it is worth considering the establishment of similar projects elsewhere.

A longer-term solution involves working with established disability organisations towards the eventual provision of a national disability income as of right. Both DIG and the Disability Alliance have put forward proposals for such a scheme, and while both organisations would argue that their proposals are radically different, to the outsider they look broadly similar. Part of the conflict may stem from the fact that the Alliance is part of the 'poverty lobby' and thus to the left politically, whereas DIG is avowedly non-political.

Not all organisations are united in this 'incomes approach' to disability. The Union of the Physically Impaired Against Segregation suggests that poverty is a symptom of disabled people's oppression and not the cause and consequently it may be inappropriate to attack the symptom without dealing with the cause. UPIAS advances three fundamental principles:

disability is a social situation, caused by social conditions, which requires for its elimination

(a) that no one aspect such as incomes, mobility, or institutions is treated in isolation
(b) that disabled people should, with the help and advice of others, assume control over their own lives, and

(c) that professionals, experts and others who seek to help must be committed to promoting such control by disabled people.

(UPIAS, 1976, p. 3)

It could be argued that financial benefits fall within the province of the DHSS and that therefore social workers should not get involved. However, there are two arguments that can counter this: it is clear that the DHSS cannot be relied on to ensure that disabled people get their entitlements; and as poverty is a major problem for many disabled people, it is an abrogation of professional responsibility not to make any attempt to alleviate it. Both individual welfare rights advice, provided it is accurate, and the establishment of welfare rights projects, are thus part of the social work task. Involvement in the incomes approach to disability, however, is a personal rather than professional responsibility, and while social workers may join organisations in their spare time active involvement in the politics of disability is perhaps beyond their professional duty.

The rights of disabled people: ways forward?

It is clear then that disabled people do currently have rights: legally enshrined rights not to be discriminated against in the employment market, the right to education commensurate with need, and the right to a whole range of benefits and services. However, it is plain that many disabled people do not get these rights and there are raging arguments about how best the rights of disabled people should be safeguarded and extended. I have characterised these arguments elsewhere (Oliver, M., 1982) as 'persuasion versus enforcement' or 'the carrot versus the stick'. The persuasionist view suggests that discrimination against disabled people arises as the result of either negative attitudes or the failure to consider particular 'special' needs. From this point of view what is needed is more information, public education campaigns and research. This position is exemplified by the Manpower Services Commission in its approach to the employment right of disabled people.

The enforcement view, on the other hand, suggests that strong legal action is necessary, for it is only then that disabled people will achieve their rights. There are three problems with this view, however:

(a) Even if legislation is passed, it may not be enforced — the Disabled Persons (Employment) Act 1944 is a good example of this.
(b) Even if legislation is passed and enforced, it may not achieve its aim of ending discrimination. Both the Equal Pay and Race Relations Acts are examples of this.
(c) Such legislation tends to operate to the benefit of certain sections of the professional classes rather than serve to protect the interests of all the groups for whom the legislation was designed.

(Oliver, M., 1982, p. 78)

Thus it has been suggested by Shearer (1981b) that what is needed is some additional anti-discrimination legislation. This call for anti-discrimination legislation has been picked up by a number of disabled people and their organisations, based largely upon the apparent success of such legislation for disabled people in the USA. The Committee on Restrictions against Disabled People (CORAD, 1982) has published a report strongly advocating the need for just such legislation in all areas where disabled people may experience discrimination of whatever kind.

One other important development in recent years is the growing political power of disabled people and the effect that this may have on policy provision for disabled people in the future. There are a number of exciting developments occurring. In Britain there has been formed a National Council of Organisations of Disabled People, and in 1981 this national body sent representatives to the Disabled Persons International in Singapore. It is from this growing consciousness and political power of disabled people that ultimately solutions to the problems of disability may emerge.

In conclusion, it may be impossible for social workers as professionals to participate in the growing political movement of disabled people, though there may be scope for working with these emergent organisations. However, this will have implications for the 'professional attitude' to professional practice in general and disabled people in particular, and it is a theme which will be considered further in the final chapter. Clearly, however, there are a number of important social work tasks to be tackled in a society not totally committed to the ultimate goal of removing the disabling consequences of impairment.

7
Conclusions: Some Professional and Organisational Aspects of Social Work with Disabled People

This final chapter will attempt to bring together some of the issues thrown up by attempting to apply the social model of disability to social work as an organised professional activity. It will begin by considering some of the professional aspects of the matter by asking questions about the nature of the professional task: Who should do it? What kinds of qualifications and training are needed? Consideration will then be given to the organisational context in which social work with disabled people actually takes place and the constraints this may impose upon professional activity. Finally, implications for the future will be considered.

Models of social work practice with disabled people

A major problem in developing an adequate conceptualisation of social work practice in this area is that there are few, if any, existing models or frameworks adequate for the purpose. One attempt to devise a comprehensive scheme was made by the Working Party which produced the CCETSW Report *People with Handicaps Need Better Trained Workers* (see Table 7.1).

This scheme is an honourable attempt to relate levels of

Table 7.1 *Training related to clients' needs*

	Group A	Group B	Group C	
Clients	All handicapped without 'special' needs but requiring workers to be alert to part played by handicap in presenting problem (e.g. each may aggravate the other)	Handicapped with 'special' needs arising from nature/ consequences or developmental stage of handicap	Severely disabled with 'extra' needs (e.g. profoundly deaf or severely subnormal)	
Workers	Senior workers on intake and assessment	Senior workers as advisors	Senior Workers as consultants	Trainers Consultants Managers Planners
	Basic-grade field and residential workers in hospital and health services, local authority social services depts, voluntary agencies, probation and after-care service	Basic-grade workers as in (A) but interested in and developing skills to help with problems related to handicaps	Basic-grade workers as in (A) but with additional technical skills	
	As workers become more knowledgeable and skilled they become 'special' resource, point of reference, adviser, consultant, etc.			
Training	Improved teaching *re* disabled and handicaps in all CQSW courses, or for those who did not get this, day-release or block short courses providing similar teaching	Short courses of varying length and pattern providing additional training with high input of content *re* specific conditions — comparative studies and acquisition of some additional skills in order to meet 'special' needs of clients.	Courses of suitable length providing further additional training — study of one particular handicap in depth — acquisition of technical skills where needed to meet the 'extra' needs of clients (e.g. communication)	
		Advanced courses *re* handicap or other advanced course		

Source: CCETSW (1974, p. 29).

disability both to work expertise and necessary level of training. There are, however, a number of problems. No real attempt is made to distinguish between client groups A, B and C or to explain differences between 'special' and 'extra' needs. The attempt to construct a worker-skill scale which relates to these different groups of disabled people assumes a fairly mechanical relationship between the needs of clients and the skills possessed by professionals. However, the most serious criticism of all is that the conceptualisation of disability within the scheme is a limited one based upon the individual rather than the social model. It assumes that there is a direct relationship between the extent of impairment, the level of need in the client and thereby the professional skills that should be made available. The social model, however, suggests that there is no such direct relationship: someone with a very severe impairment may only be mildly disabled, whereas someone with a minor impairment may be totally disabled by poverty, poor housing, the attitudes of employers or hostile social treatment. A scarce resource like professional expertise should be allocated on the extent of disability, not on the extent of impairment as suggested by the CCETSW scheme.

Another attempt to establish the social work task in relation to social work practice with disabled people stems from the BASW 'Guidelines' (1982). These take as their starting-point the specific roles identified in BASW's *The Social Work Task* (1977) and then consider in detail the application of those roles which should only normally be performed by an appropriately qualified worker to working with disabled people. The roles identified are diagnostician, planner, director, counsellor, attitude/behaviour changer and consultant. The major problem with this approach is, as the 'Guidelines' themselves recognise:

> Given the generic nature of social work education it is clearly unrealistic to expect all newly qualified social workers to have acquired, in the course of their professional training, a great deal of specific knowledge of and experience in working with disabled clients or their families.

(BASW, 1982, p. 31)

It is perhaps therefore not unrealistic to assume that, without appropriate knowledge and experience, the roles identified could not be performed even by qualified social workers.

Neither of these two attempts to lay a professional basis for the practice of social work with disabled people really comes to grips with the perennial problem of the relationship between theory and practice, knowledge and skill. It should be stressed, however, that the individual and social models of disability are dependent upon that relationship, either overtly or covertly. Thus it could be said that the individual model stems from the 'personal tragedy theory of disability', whereas the social model stems from 'the social problem theory of disability'. This perennial problem is thus a crucial factor in the failure of social work to provide an adequate professional base for its work with disabled people.

An attempt to look at this problem in the context of social work generally has been made by Lee (in Bailey and Lee, 1982, p. 16), who distinguishes between three levels:

Level 1   *Actual task*
Level 2   *Technical knowledge*
Level 3   *Theoretical knowledge*

While, ideally, good social work practice should be based upon an integration of all three levels, in reality there is often a polarisation between 'academics' and 'practitioners', with each group seeing its sphere of activity as unrelated to the other. Lee, however, suggests that 'speculative theory with scant regard for practice (level 1) is of little utility, and practice insulated from theoretical questions (level 3) while perfectly permissible in car maintenance, is downright dangerous in social work' (in Bailey and Lee, 1982, p. 17).

The problem with both the CCETSW and BASW attempts to establish a framework is that they have almost totally been concerned with the relationship between levels 1 and 2, whereas both the social model of disability and this book are concerned primarily with the relationship between levels 2 and 3. There are a number of reasons for this. Articulated theories about disability are few and far between, as are considerations of their relationship to technical knowledge. Also, it is extremely difficult to draw up a skills manual for social workers which is not the same as drawing up a skills manual for plumbers, electricians or car mechanics. Finally, much work with disabled people has been a theoretical, either based covertly upon the individual model of disability, or simply orientated to the immediate practical task at hand. This approach has problems, for, as Lee has argued:

> theory must have regard for practice but it should not be 'tailored' for it. Practical contingencies must not be allowed to dictate the terms of theoretical speculation, for if they do a most anaemic form of theorising will result. Such theory, raised in a protected environment to fit necessity, is the stuff of car maintenance manuals; and people informed by such manuals might be able to perform reasonably efficiently, but then so could un-reflexive automatons.
>
> (in Bailey and Lee, 1982, p. 41)

Suggesting that the social model of disability provides an adequate and appropriate base for developing social work practice with disabled people does not resolve the issue of whether such practice might be conservative or radical. Indeed, it is perfectly possible to suggest that the parallels between this social model and the unitary approach to social work practice are so close that all that is necessary is to increase the knowledge of disability to social workers already trained in this unitary approach for social work with disabled people to become an established part of professional practice.

This view, however, does not take into account the organisational pressures which limit professional activity with disabled clients in social services departments as they are currently organised. Furthermore, it does not take into account that the unitary approach, based upon systems theory, is inherently conservative and does not challenge existing social relations. Deeply embedded as it is in social consciousness generally, the individual model or personal disaster theory of disability can only be replaced or superseded by a radical change in both theoretical conceptualisation and practical approach.

If this is the case, and I have argued strongly that it is, then it has fundamental implications both for the training needs of social workers and for the professional organisation of generic social work. It is not enough merely to increase knowledge about disability on basic training courses; this must be tackled alongside a reversion towards specialist practice and away from the generic approach. This is in fact implicit in the scheme advanced by the CCETSW referred to earlier in the chapter. (I am grateful to Graham Willetts for this suggestion.)

The problems of both organisational orientation and professional commitment to work with disabled people are rooted in the reorganisation of local authorities and the post-Seebohm creation of social services departments. Satyamurti describes the experience in the department she studied:

> As the time of reorganisation drew nearer, CCOs [child care officers] began to feel more anxiety at the prospect of it. Many of them felt distaste at the idea of working with elderly and physically handicapped people, or were worried about having to deal with the mentally ill. Others felt not so much distaste as a sense that their professional status would be eroded by having to do 'welfare-type' work. As one qualified CCO put it, 'I didn't do social work training in order to sit and have friendly chats with lonely old ladies.' Many were concerned at the possibility of being overwhelmed by the huge caseloads coming from the Welfare Department and were pessimistic about maintaining standards of work. Welfare Department social workers, for their part, discerned that both they and their clients were despised by the Children's Department, and felt that they would be subordinated in the new department to a 'child care' way of doing things. For both groups, part of the anxiety centred on the question of who would get the senior and management positions in the new department — from which former disciplines would they be drawn?

> (Satyamurti, 1981, p. 20)

It is clear that child care is given priority, but this is not solely due to the fact that it was, on the whole, former child-care specialists who achieved most of the managerial positions in the new departments. There are other organisational pressures which 'trap' social workers as well as their clients in particular forms of social relations engendered by welfare bureaucracies. It is to some of these that consideration now needs to be given, and in the terms used in this book it could be argued that social workers themselves are often 'disabled' in their day-to-day practice with disabled people.

The organisational context of social work practice

The constraints upon social workers do not stem simply from the departments within which they work, but also from the relationship between the needs of disabled people and the allocation of scarce resources. The issue of the relationship between the needs of disabled people and the services provided is a complicated one in which there is no direct link between the two. The complexities of the relationship can best be illustrated by means of a diagram (see Figure 7.1).

From the diagram it is clear that there is no direct relationship between the needs of disabled people and the services they receive. Rather, disabled people have their needs defined and interpreted by others, and the services provided to meet these needs are often delivered by large, bureaucratic organisations. Where the crucial problem is to ration scarce resources among competing demands, social workers and social work training are not necessarily the most suited to this particular role.

The experiences of social workers when working for the Family Fund are, in microcosm, the experiences of many social workers in social services departments. Bradshaw describes some of the dilemmas:

the discretion of the social worker in the Fund's offices in York began to be constrained by pressure of work and the Panel's decisions. The rising number of applications and cases pending soon made it very difficult for social workers to spend the time needed to carry out the detailed inquiries upon which their discretion had to be used. Alarmed by the backlog, the Fund's managers began to introduce routine procedures and to urge social workers to reduce the time spent on each case. Routine cases were given to unqualified staff and all were urged to confine themselves to the item requested and not 'try to do casework at a distance'. The social workers, feeling that the problem arose as a result of delays in recruiting staff, were unwilling to accept limits imposed on their professional judgment, and they were not happy in seeing needs that they had recognised go unmet because they did not have the time to intervene. The tensions arising from these restraints on the exercise of professional discretion and the need to speed up the making of grants continued throughout the phase of exploratory development; they were heightened further by the body

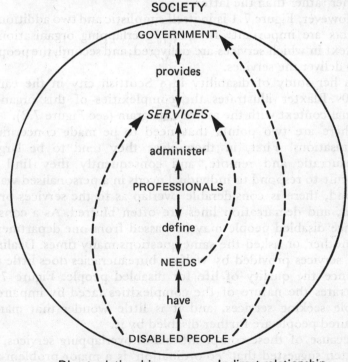

Key: —— Direct relationship ---- Indirect relationship

Source: Oliver, M. (1982, p. 57).

Figure 7.1 *The relationship between needs and services*

of rules that began to emerge from the Panel about what kind of help could be given, and from the Medical Advisory Panel about which children were eligible.

(Bradshaw, 1980, p. 41)

As a consequence of this social workers tended to leave the Fund and were gradually replaced by administrators. The problem for social workers in social services departments, however, is not merely one of lack of opportunities to work in different ways elsewhere, but is also exacerbated by the failure of the profession to distinguish between professional and administrative criteria for decision-making, and further to support workers who wish to make decisions based on the former rather than the latter.

However, Figure 7.1 is in itself simplistic and two additional aspects are important: first, the overlapping organisational context in which services are delivered; and second, the people who deliver the services.

In her study of disability in a Scottish city in the early 1970s Blaxter illustrates the complexities of this organisational context with the aid of a diagram (see Figure 7.2).

There are two points that need to be made concerning organisations. First, in themselves they tend to be large, bureaucratic and remote, and consequently they find it difficult to respond to individual needs in a personalised way. Second, there is considerable overlap as to the services provided, and demarcation lines are often blurred. As a consequence disabled people may be passed from one department to another, or asked the same questions many times. Dealing with services provided by welfare bureaucracies does little to enhance the quality of life for disabled people. Figure 7.2 illustrates the nature of the complexities faced by impaired people seeking services, and it is little wonder that many impaired people are further disabled by it.

Because of these complexities and overlapping services, it is often suggested that 'co-ordination' is a major problem in providing services for disabled people. To overcome this, the idea of a *named person* has been suggested in a number of government reports (Court, Warnock), and this suggestion is

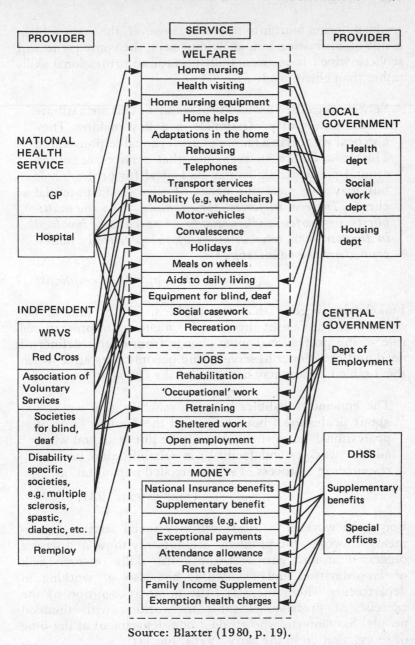

Source: Blaxter (1980, p. 19).

Figure 7.2 *Services for disabled people in one city*

gradually being built into practice. However, the real problem is not co-ordination but, as Wilding says, the consequences of services which have been built up around professional skills rather than client need:

> Services organised around professional skills are a tribute to the power of professionals in policy making. They also bear witness to a failure of professional responsibility. This is a failure to recognise that services organised around particular skills may be logical for professionals but may not meet the needs of clients and potential clients. *The real sufferers, for example, from the multiplicity of professionals actually or potentially involved in the care and rehabilitation of the physically handicapped are the handicapped.*
>
> (Wilding, 1982, p. 98, *my emphasis*)

Finkelstein suggests that the problem is not one of co-ordination but one of the need for a change in professional role — the professional must change from expert definer of need and/or rationer of services and become a resource which the disabled person may use as he or she chooses:

> The endemic squabbles between rehabilitation workers about professional boundaries and the familiar farce of professional 'teamwork' can only be put at an end when all the workers and facilities in rehabilitation become resources in a process of self-controlled rehabilitation.
>
> (Finkelstein, 1981, p. 27)

For social workers in local authority social services departments, however, the problems are not only those of a service organised around narrow professional skills or even lack of co-ordination and teamwork, but also of working in departments where there is little or no recognition of the exercise of professional skills in working with disabled people. Satyamurti, who studied one department at the time of reorganisation in the early 1970s, suggests:

It tended to be the case that higher priority was given to family cases than to old people or the physically handicapped, but this was a result of common perspectives and common pressures impinging on each individual social worker, and not the result of a decision that this should be the case. This lack of clear direction from above can be seen as partly responsible for social workers' chronic state of unease and anxiety about what they were doing, and the pervasive feeling that they were never doing enough.

(Satyamurti, 1981, p. 32)

Thus it can be argued that Seebohm did not create generic departments but specialist child-care ones, where the needs of children were met by trained professionals and other needs and obligations were met by unqualified staff, welfare assistants, and the like.

With regard to the people who deliver services, the disabled person may be confronted with more than a dozen different professionals. Brechin and Liddiard have recently compiled a list of 'helpers', which is reproduced here to give an indication of the numbers of paid workers who may be involved in the lives of disabled people:

Helpers of the Disabled

1. Audiology Technician
2. Chiropodist
3. Clinical Psychologist
4. Community Nurses for the Mentally Handicapped
5. Dietitian
6. Disablement Resettlement Officer
7. District Nurse
8. Doctors
9. Educational Psychologist
10. Educational Welfare Officer
11. General Nurse
12. Health Visitor
13. Occupational Therapist
14. Orthoptist
15. Physiotherapist

16. Remedial Gymnast
17. Self Help and Parent Action Groups
18. Social Work and Social Service
     (a) Social Worker
     (b) Social Work Assistants
     (c) Organisers of Home Helps and Volunteers
     (d) Care Staff in Residential Homes, Hostels and
         Special Schools
     (e) Managers, Senior Staff and Instructors in Day
         Services
     (f) Specialist Workers with the Handicapped
     (g) Mobility Officers and Technical Workers with
         Visually Handicapped People
     (h) Home Helps
19. Community Workers
20. Specialist Careers Officers
21. Speech Therapists
22. Teachers of
     (a) Physically and Mentally Handicapped Children
     (b) Mentally Handicapped Adults
     (c) Remedial Teachers
23. Voluntary Workers.

(Brechin and Liddiard, 1981, p. 138)

A major problem for disabled people and their families is
very often not just a matter of which particular agency to
approach but also of which particular professional to contact.
Furthermore, even when professionals are in contact, disabled
people and their families are often unclear which department
the professional represents and consequently what services
may, or may not, be offered. One way out of this dilemma
has been suggested by numerous government reports (Court,
1976; Warnock, 1978) that a 'named person' should be
appointed both to serve as an immediate contact point and a
co-ordinator of services. This idea has been widely welcomed
and enshrined in recent legislation (e.g. the Education Act
1981).

However, there are a number of problems related to the
idea, particularly about whether the named person will in

fact be the 'key worker' or simply someone given nominal responsibility, like the head of a special school. There is also the question about whether most professionals have sufficient knowledge and skills to act in this capacity, and both in terms of their strategic position and Finkelstein's principle of self-controlled rehabilitation the *disabled person* is the most logical choice as both named person and key worker. The professional task, therefore, should not be to usurp the key worker position from the disabled person but rather work with him or her to ensure that the required knowledge is acquired. This will allay the by no means groundless fears that in a few years' time a new profession of 'named persons' will have arisen with its own career structure, salary increments and enhanced professional status.

There are a number of other problems to which the professional relationship may give rise. McKnight (1981) has suggested that the very relationship is itself disabling, and others (Robinson, 1978; Fox, 1974) have pointed to the fact that very often professional definitions of need do not co-incide with needs defined by disabled people themselves. Consequently where professional and personal definitions of need conflict, the quality of life for disabled people is unlikely to be enhanced. Scott, who has written perceptively on the topic, states that the professional

> has been specially trained to give professional help to impaired people. He cannot use his expertise if those who are sent to him for assistance do not regard themselves as being impaired. Given this fact, it is not surprising that the doctrine has emerged among experts that truly effective rehabilitation and adjustment can occur only after the client has squarely faced and accepted the 'fact' that he is, indeed, 'impaired'.
>
> (Scott, 1970, p. 280)

And it is not just in terms of 'acceptance of disability' but also in the assessment of needs and services that professionals seek to impose their definitions, though not always with total success. Thus many disabled people have their needs met (or not) by professionalised welfare bureaucracies which very often may not provide the appropriate service in an acceptable fashion. This does not mean that the welfare state has to be dismantled, as some would like, as there are a few less drastic solutions.

Some ways forward?

The first answer involves some movement away from the delivery of health and personal services through a profession-alised bureaucracy. As a recent Minister of Health commented, 'Health is not just something that is provided for by the NHS, but that each individual has a responsibility for his own well being' (Owen, 1976).

The Chronically Sick and Disabled Persons Act has been criticised for taking away from the individual responsibility for his or her own life-style:

> The goodwill behind the 1970 Act's provision cannot be doubted. But the philosophy can, for what it does is to reinforce the notion that people who happen to have disabilities are people who are 'helpless', unable to choose for themselves the aid to opportunity they need. What this effectively does is to lock them into service providers' perception of what is good for them, and so limit rather than expand their areas of effective choice.
>
> (Shearer, 1981b, p. 82)

Shearer's solution to this problem is to provide more cash rather than services, but asserts that this by itself would not be enough and that such provision must be reinforced by anti-discrimination legislation to guarantee disabled people the right to participate fully in all aspects of their lives.

Participation by disabled people was an idea built into the 1970 Act through sections 9–15. Section 15 imposed a blanket requirement on local authorities to appoint at least one disabled person to all committees not restricted to officers and members alone. However, some ten years later the DHSS has been unable to produce any evidence as to implementation:

The degree to which Section 15 has had any effect on participation in community affairs of disabled people must, therefore, remain a mystery. Doubts about the extent to which disabled people are involved in local authority committee work reduce the confidence with which we might assume that their views are fully considered when local authorities plan priorities and implement economies that affect their welfare.

(Topliss and Gould, 1981, p. 132)

There are two other areas in which participation could be important. To begin with, disabled people could participate in the provision of services, but there is no evidence that health and welfare bureaucracies fulfil their obligations under the 1944 Employment (Disabled Persons) Act to employ a minimum 3 per cent of disabled workers. The other level of participation is in the professional/client relationship, already referred to. Whether in this area this participation should be on an equal basis, or whether the disabled person should be the master and the professional the servant, is a matter of some debate.

Regardless of whether one favours professional or client control, it is clear that not only are disabled people demanding new forms of professional practice, but many professionals are also discontented with the roles they are expected to play and tasks they are expected to perform. This is evidenced by a variety of calls for providing adequate training to help professionals develop new forms of practice to meet changing needs, including the CCETSW Report (1974) already discussed, the Jay Report (1979) and the Royal Commission on the National Health Service (1979). Disabled people, too, are specifying the directions in which practice must move:

The basis of professional practice must rest on an assumption of integration and a commitment to promoting control by disabled people over their own lives. Since the lives of disabled people also depend on the actions of helpers, control over education, training and role of such helpers needs to be vested in disabled people (quite aside from the need for more disabled people to enter the profession).

What this means in practice is that the role of the professional worker in rehabilitation, for example, needs to change from management of the patient to that of being a resource for the patient to use in reaching his or her own goals. The suggestion that professional workers in rehabilitation should become a resource to be utilised by disabled people is not a suggestion that professionals should become passive and all the onus for innovation, assessment, decision-making, etc. should fall on the shoulders of disabled people. Professionals acting as a resource to be used by others need special education and training so that they are able to *promote* control by disabled people.

(Finkelstein, 1981, p. 26)

Partly as a response to this lack of participation, many disabled people have begun to investigate and develop alternative possibilities. Specifically with regard to disability, once a medical condition has been stabilised, there is no reason why disabled people should not take responsibility for their health, just as everyone else does. Indeed, a number of disability organisations are concerned in the area of self-help and health (Robinson and Henry, 1977). Furthermore, disabled people and their organisations are not just restricting their activities to health, but are also extending them to the social consequences of disability and are banding together in order to gain access to much needed support services.

Elsewhere (Oliver, M., 1982) I have suggested that the growing number of organisations of and for disabled people can be classified in terms of one of four particular approaches: the partnership approach, the income approach, the self-help approach, and the populist approach. The partnership approach developed first and there are a large number of voluntary organisations like the Royal Association of Disability and Rehabilitation, the Spastics Society and the Cheshire Foundation which provide services for disabled people. The range of services provided is similar to the ones provided by statutory agencies, though usually care is taken not to duplicate provision — hence the *partnership*. In the late 1960s and early 1970s two other types of group began to spring up. First, there were groups like the Disablement Income Group and the Disability Alliance concerned to tackle the issue of poverty and disability — hence the *income* approach. Second, and partly as a consequence of the failure of the partnership approach and organisations for disabled people to meet the needs of disabled people as they themselves defined them, *self-help* and *populist* approaches developed.

The crucial difference between these two approaches is that self-help groups have tended to organise around particular clinical conditions or problems, as with the Spinal Injuries Association or the Association of Disabled Professionals, for example. Populist groups like the Union of the Physically Impaired Against Segregation, the National Federation of the Blind and the National Union of the Deaf have taken particular clinical conditions or problems for granted and have been much more concerned to set up democratic organisations controlled by their membership. Further, it is largely groups who are organising on a self-help or populist basis who are calling for more participation, changed professional practice and ultimately the removal of the disabling aspects of impairment.

One crucial dimension that has recently emerged in disability organisations is the distinction between organisations *of* disabled people and organisations *for* disabled people. According to one commentator:

> Organisations for the disabled outnumber organisations of disabled people by 100 to 1 and disabled people are missing from the governing bodies of the former and from their workforce. Moreover, organisations for the disabled, which proudly represent the interests of disabled people to government — and are used and supported by government for this purpose — often lack direct contact with disabled people, and are often very inadequately accountable to them.
>
> (Large, 1981, p. 6)

This division widened when in 1981 the British Council of Organisations of Disabled People wrote an open letter to Lord Snowden, asking him not to agree to act as Chairman of the Snowden Council, a proposed umbrella organisation for disabled people.

While undoubtedly disputes like this will continue, trends seem to indicate that organisations of disabled people will be an increasingly potent force. Consequently professionals, including social workers, will need to build links with such organisations and develop the skills necessary to work in ways radically different from those needed with organisations following the partnership approach.

Very often the response of professionals when confronted with patients or clients who assert the right to control their own bodies or social circumstances is to doubt their capacity to cope and also to feel vaguely threatened by such self-assertiveness. However, there are two positive aspects to this. To begin with many disabled people are more aware than anyone else of their physical conditions and the social consequences of them simply as a result of experiencing them every single day of their lives. And further, the taking of responsibility by patients or clients removes, or at least decreases, the burden of responsibility upon the professional.

No doubt at present in many professional/client interactions mutual sharing of responsibility takes place. However, the first crucial task of the 1980s must be to create organisational structures which facilitate this shift in responsibility so that services are flexibly geared to the needs of the patient/client. And the second crucial task must be to alter professional practice so that it is the disabled person who is in control and not the social worker or another professional. Social work practice with disabled people must move in these directions if it is not to be inadequate, unsatisfactory, uninspired and ultimately demeaning both for the social worker and the disabled person.

This book was mainly written before the publication of the Barclay Report, but it is interesting to note that three of the essential social work tasks there identified — social care planning, community social work and counselling — are the three most important tasks identified here. Not only that, but following the social model of disability this book has placed emphasis upon material resources while not denying the importance of emotional support. The Barclay Report came to similar conclusions:

> The emphasis by physically handicapped people was very much on material help. But they recognised the need for support and help in coming to terms with handicap and for families in coping with the emotional stresses and tensions within marriages to which dependence or handicap may give rise.
>
> (Barclay Committee, 1982, p. 163)

I hope that this book and the Barclay Report provide a framework against which to provide more effective services for and with disabled people and offer the possibility of making the relationships between disabled people and social workers more effective and fruitful for all concerned than they have been up to now.

A Guide to Further Reading

Chapter 1

The social mode of disability, though not necessarily called that, is well articulated by Shearer (1981a). Further dimensions are added in a collection of readings (Brechin *et al.*, 1981) produced for the Open University. Finally, Sutherland (1981) encapsulates the social model in describing his and other disabled people's experiences of living in a hostile social world.

Chapter 2

The OPCS (Harris, 1971) survey provides a useful discussion of impairment, disability and handicap. This has subsequently been refined and developed by the World Health Organisation (1980). Finkelstein (1980) provides a stimulating counter to these definitions, and both Townsend (1979) and Blaxter (1980) provide useful discussions of the problems of definitions in relation to their own particular studies.

Chapter 3

Both Blaxter (1980) and Carver (1982) use the concept of 'career' in relation to disabled people. Taylor (1977) attempts to discuss the medical and social dimensions of disability, though he ends up by stressing the importance of medicine — perhaps a useful counter to this book. Halliburton and Quelch (1981) have produced a useful guide to the medical and other information that social workers need to know. Finally, both Bell and Klemz (1981) and Brechin and Liddiard (1981) list the services available to disabled people, though the latter work is superior both in terms of information and approach.

Chapter 4

The book by Lonsdale *et al.* (1979) is the most comprehensive attempt so far to relate the principles and practices of social work intervention to families with a disabled child. While not always logically consistent, it is essential reading for all social workers working in such situations. Robinson's (1978) account of the relationship between professionals and clients is also well worth reading. On sexual aspects of disability Stewart's (1979) work is probably still the best available. Both of the EOC Reports (1982a, 1982b) capture the problems of living with an elderly disabled relative, and Swain (1982) provides the most thorough and well-balanced overall discussion of family life where there is a disabled member.

Chapter 5

Goldsmith (1976) provides what is still the most comprehensive and detailed discussion of residential care and its alternatives. Dartington *et al.* (1981) describe a number of interesting alternatives to residential care, though their account is somewhat spoilt by the intrusion of their own attitudes. Finally, Tuckey and Tuckey (1981) lay down a detailed blue-print for how day centres should be run, based upon their own experience. Another interesting set of guidelines are the principles of residential care laid down by Hampden-Inskip (1981) for the Cheshire Foundation, though it is doubtful whether any Cheshire homes follow these principles.

Chapter 6

Topliss (1979) and Topliss and Gould (1981) examine the effectiveness of the Chronically Sick and Disabled Persons Act, though the most penetrating critique is provided by Shearer (1981b). The report on the attempt to enforce the Act (Cook and Mitchell, 1982) also makes interesting reading. The CORAD Report (1982) documents the extent of discrimination against disabled people and makes forty-two recommendations, including an endorsement of the need for anti-discrimination legislation. All social workers should possess and use the most recent copy of the *Disability Rights Handbook* produced by the Disability Alliance.

Chapter 7

Until BASW finally publishes its 'Guidelines on social work with people with disabilities', the most comprehensive discussion of professional and organisational issues is still the CCETSW Report (1974). Satyamurti (1981) shows why 'doing social work' with disabled people is difficult and unpopular in the current organisational context. Finally, Finkelstein (1981) provides the most lucid proposal for developing new relationships between rehabilitation professionals and their disabled clients.

Bibliography

Abrams, P. (1978) 'Community care: some research problems and priorities', in Barnes and Connelly (1978).

Albrecht, G. L. (ed.) (1976) *The Sociology of Physical Disability and Rehabilitation*, University of Pittsburgh Press.

Albrecht, G. and Levy, J. (1981) 'Constructing disabilities as social problems', in G. Albrecht (ed.), *Cross National Rehabilitation Policies: A Sociological Perspective*, Beverly Hills, Sage.

Anderson, D. (1982) *Social Work and Mental Handicap*, London, Macmillan.

Bailey, R. and Lee, P. (ed.) (1982) *Theory and Practice in Social Work*, Oxford, Blackwell.

Baird, P. (1980) 'The last word', *Social Work Today*, 19 August.

Barclay Committee (1982) *Social Workers: Their Role and Tasks*, London, Bedford Square Press.

Barnes, J. and Connelly, N. (eds) (1978) *Social Care Research*, London, Bedford Square Press.

Barton, R. (1959) *Institutional Neurosis*, London, John Wright.

Battye, L. (1966) 'The Chatterley syndrome', in P. Hunt (ed.), *Stigma*, London, Geoffrey Chapman.

Becker, H. (1963) *Outsiders: Studies in the Sociology of Deviance*, New York, Free Press.

Bell, L. and Klemz, A. (1981) *Physical Handicap*, Cambridge, Woodhead-Faulkner.

Blaxter, M. (1980) *The Meaning of Disability*, 2nd edn, London, Heinemann.

Bloomfield, R. (1976) 'Younger chronic sick units: a survey and critique', unpublished paper.

Booth, T. (1981) 'Demystifying integration', in W. Swann (ed.), *The Practice of Special Education*, Oxford, Blackwell in association with the Open University Press.

Boswell, D. M. and Wingrove, J. M. (eds) (1974) *The Handicapped Person in the Community*, London, Tavistock.

Bradshaw, J. (1980) *The Handicapped Child and His Family. The Family Fund: An Initiative in Social Policy*, London, Routledge & Kegan Paul.

Brechin, A., Liddiard, P. and Swain, J. (eds) (1981) *Handicap in a Social World*, London, Hodder & Stoughton.

Brechin, A. and Liddiard, P. (1981) *Look at this Way: New Perspectives in Rehabilitation*, London, Hodder & Stoughton.

Brewer, C. and Lait, J. (1980) *Can Social Work Survive?*, London, Temple Smith.

British Association of Social Workers (1982) 'Guidelines for social work with the disabled', draft paper, London, BASW.

Buckle, J. (1971) *Work and Housing of Impaired People in Great Britain*, London, HMSO.

Burgess, P. (1982) 'In benefit', *Community Care*, 1 July 1982.

Campling, J. (ed.) (1982) *The Handicapped Person — A New Perspective for Social Workers?*, London, RADAR.

Carroll, T. J. (1961) *Blindness — what it is, what it does, and how to live with it*, Boston, Little, Brown.

Carter, J. (1981) *Day Services for Adults*, London, Allen & Unwin.

Carver, V. (1982) *The Individual Behind the Statistics*, Milton Keynes, Open University Press.

Casserly, J. and Clark, B. (1978) *A Welfare Rights Approach to the Chronically Sick and Disabled*, Strathclyde Regional Council.

CCETSW (1974) *Social Work: People with Handicaps Need Better Trained Workers*, London, Central Council for Education and Training in Social Work.

Clark, F. le Gros (1969) *Blinded in War: A Model for the Welfare of all Handicapped People*, Herts, Wayland.

Cook, J. and Mitchell, P. (1982) *Putting Teeth in the Act: A History of Attempts to Enforce the Provisions of Section 2 of the Chronically Sick and Disabled Persons Act 1970*, London, RADAR.

CORAD (1982) *Report by the Committee on Restrictions Against Disabled People*, London, HMSO.

Corrigan, P. and Leonard, P. (1979) *Social Work Practice Under Capitalism*, London, Macmillan.

Court Report (1976) *Fit for the Future: The Report of the Committee on Child Health Services*, London, HMSO.

Cypher, J. (ed.) (1979) *Seebohm Across Three Decades*, London, BASW.

Dartington, T., Miller, E. and Gwynne, G. (1981) *A Life Together*, London, Tavistock.

Davis, K. (1981) '28–38 Grove Road: accommodation and care in a community setting', in Brechin *et al.* (1981).

Davis K. and Woodward, J. (1981) 'DIAL UK: development of the National Association of Disablement Information and Advice Services', in Brechin *et al.* (1981).

De Jong, G. (1981) 'The movement for independent living: origins, ideology and implications for disability research', in Brechin *et al.* (1981).

Department of Health and Social Security (1968) *Report of the Committee on Local Authority and Allied Social Services*, Seebohm Report, London, HMSO.

Department of Health and Social Security (1976) *The Way Forward: Priorities for Health and Personal Social Services in England*, London, HMSO.

Department of Health and Social Security (1981) *Care in Action*, London, HMSO.

Dickinson, M. (1977) 'Rehabilitating the traumatically disabled adult', *Social Work Today*, vol. 8, no. 28.

Douglas, J. (ed.) (1970) *Deviance and Respectability: The Social Construction of Moral Meanings*, New York, BASK Books.

Doyal, L. (1980) *The Political Economy of Health*, London, Pluto Press.

Equal Opportunities Commission (1982a) *Caring for the Elderly and Handicapped*, London, EOC.

Equal Opportunities Commission (1982b) *Who Cares for the Carers? Opportunities for those Caring for the Elderly and Handicapped*, London, EOC.

Farber, B. (1975) 'Family adaptations to severely retarded children', in M. Begab and S. Richardson (eds), *The Mentally Retarded and Society: A Social Science Perspective*, Chicago, University Park Press.

Finkelstein, V. (1980) *Attitudes and Disabled People: Issues for Discussion*, New York, World Rehabilitation Fund.

Finkelstein, V. (1981) *Disability and Professional Attitudes*, Sevenoaks, NAIDEX Convention.

Finlay, B. (1978) *Housing and Disability: A Report on the Housing Needs of Physically Handicapped People in Rochdale*, Rochdale Voluntary Action.

Fitzgerald, R. G. (1970) 'Reaction to blindness: an exploratory study of adults', *Archives of General Psychiatry*, vol. 22, April, Chicago, American Medical Association.

Fox, A. M. (1974) *They get this training but they don't really know how you feel*, London, RADAR.

Glendinning, C. (1981) *Resource Worker Project: Final Report*, Social Policy Research Unit, University of York.

Goffman, E. (1961) *Asylums*, New York, Doubleday.

Goffman, E. (1963) *Stigma: Some Notes on the Management of Spoiled Identity*, Englewood Cliffs, N.J., Prentice-Hall.

Goldberg, M. and Warburton, C. (1979) *Ends and Means in Social Work*, London, Allen & Unwin.

Goldsmith, S. (1976) *Designing for the Disabled*, 3rd edn, London, Royal Institute of British Architects.

Grover, R. and Gladstone, G. (1982) *Disabled People − A Right to Work?*, London, Bedford Square Press.

Halliburton, P. and Quelch, K. (1981) *Get Help: A Guide for Social Workers to the Management of Illness in the Community*, London, Tavistock.

Hampden-Inskip, J. (1981) *Residential Homes for the Physically Handicapped*, London, Bedford Square Press.

Hanks, J. and Hanks, L. (1980) 'The physically handicapped in certain non-occidental societies', in Phillips and Rosenberg (1980).

Hanvey, C. (1981) *Social Work with Mentally Handicapped People*, London, Heinemann.

Harris, A. (1971) *Handicapped and Impaired in Great Britain*, London, IIMSO.

Hatch, S. (1980) *Outside the State*, London, Croom Helm.

Hunt, P. (1981) 'Settling accounts with the parasite people', a critique of *A Life Apart* by Miller and Gwynne, *Disability Challenge*, no. 1, UPIAS.

Ibbotson, J. (1975) 'Psychological effects of physical disability', *Occupational Therapy*, January.

Illich, I. (1975) *Medical Nemesis: The Expropriation of Health*, London, Marion Boyars.

Inkeles, A. (1964) *What is Sociology?*, Englewood Cliffs, N.J. Prentice-Hall.

Jay Report (1979) *Report of the Committee of Enquiry into Mental Handicap Nursing and Care*, London, HMSO.

Keeble, U. (1979) *Aids and Adaptations*, London, Bedford Square Press.

Knight, R. and Warren, M. (1978) *Physically Handicapped People Living at Home: A Study of Numbers and Needs*, London, HMSO.

Kuhn, T. (1962) *The Structure of Scientific Revolutions*, Chicago, University of Chicago Press.

Large, P. (1981) 'Enabling the disabled: voluntary initiative and the autonomy of disabled people', paper given to Royal College of Physicians, 1 October.

Lemert, E. (1967) *Human Deviance, Social Problems and Social Control*, Englewood Cliffs, N.J. Prentice-Hall.

Leonard, P. (1966) 'The challenge of primary prevention', *Social Work Today*, 6 October.

Lonsdale, G., Elfer, P. and Ballard, R. (1979) *Children, Grief and Social Work*, Oxford, Blackwell.

McKnight, J. (1981) 'Professionalised service and disabled help', in Brechin *et al.* (1981).

Manpower Services Commission (1981) *Review of the Quota Scheme for the Employment of Disabled People*, London, MSC.

Marshall, M. (1983) *Social Work with Old People*, London, Macmillan.

Merton, R. (1957) *Social Theory and Social Structure*, New York, Free Press.

Miller, E. and Gwynne, G. (1971) *A Life Apart*, London, Tavistock.

Musgrove, F. (1977) *Margins of the Mind*, London, Methuen.

Nissel, M. and Bonnerjea, L. (1982) *Family Care of the Handicapped Elderly: Who Pays?*, London, Policy Studies Institute.

North Surrey CHC (1978) 'Care and facilities for the younger disabled', unpublished paper.

Oliver, J. (1981) 'Caring for the handicapped family', *Community Care*, February.

Oliver, J. (1982) 'Community care: who pays?', *New Society*, 24 March.

Oliver, M. (1982) *Disablement in Society*, Milton Keynes, Open University Press.

Owen, D. (1976) article in *The Times*, February.

Owen, T. (1981) 'How Remploy's survey helped Barclay', *Community Care*, 12 November.

Parsloe, P. and Stevenson, O. (1978) *Social Services Teams: The Practitioners' View*, London, HMSO.

Payne, C. (1978) 'Working with groups in the residential setting', in N. McCaughan (ed.), *Groupwork: Learning and Practice*, London, Allen & Unwin.

Phelan, P. (1979) 'The last word', *Social Work Today*.

Phillips, H. and Glendinning, C. (1981) *Who Benefits?*, London, The Disability Alliance.

Phillips, W. and Rosenberg, J. (eds) (1980) *Social Scientists and the Physically Handicapped*, London, Arno Press.

Powles, J. (1973) 'On the limitations of modern medicine', *Science, Medicine and Man*, vol. 1.

Robinson, D. and Henry, S. (1977) *Self-Help and Health*, London, Martin Robertson.

Robinson, T. (1978) *In Worlds Apart: Professionals and their Clients in the Welfare State*, London, Bedford Square Press.

Roith, A. (1974) 'The myth of parental attitudes', in Boswell and Wingrove (1974).

Rowan, P. (1980) *What Sort of Life?*, Windsor, NFER Publishing.

Rowlings, C. (1981) *Social Work with Elderly People*, London, Allen & Unwin.

Royal Commission on the National Health Service (1979) *Report*, London, HMSO.

Ryan, J. and Thomas, F. (1980) *The Politics of Mental Handicap*, Harmondsworth, Penguin.

Safilios-Rothschild, C. (1970) *The Sociology and Social Psychology of Disability and Rehabilitation*, New York, Random House.

Sainsbury, S. (1970) *Registered as Disabled*, Occasional Papers on Social Administration No. 35, London, Bell.

Satyamurti, C. (1981) *Occupational Survival*, Oxford, Blackwell.

Scott, R. A. (1970) 'The constructions and conceptions of stigma by professional experts', in Douglas (1970).

Selfe, L. and Stow, L. (1981) *Children with Handicaps*, London, Hodder & Stoughton.

Shearer, A. (1980) *Handicapped Children in Residential Care — A Study of Policy Failure*, London, Bedford Square Press.

Shearer, A. (1981a) *Disability: Whose Handicap?*, Oxford, Blackwell.

Shearer, A. (1981b) 'A framework for independent living', in Walker and Townsend (1981).

Simkins, J. and Tickner, V. (1978) *Whose Benefit?*, London, RADAR.

Stewart, W. (1979) *The Sexual Side of Handicap*, Cambridge, Woodhead-Faulkner.

Sutherland, A. T. (1981) *Disabled We Stand*, London, Souvenir Press.

Swain, J. (1981) *Adopting a Life-Style*, Milton Keynes, Open University Press.

Swain, J. (1982) *Family Circles*, Milton Keynes, Open University Press.

Taylor, D. (1977) *Physical Impairment — Social Handicap*, London, Office of Health Economics.

Tomlinson, S. (1982) *The Sociology of Special Education*, London, Routledge & Kegan Paul.

Topliss, E. (1979) *Provision for the Disabled*, 2nd edn, Oxford, Blackwell, with Martin Robertson.

Topliss, E. and Gould, B. (1981) *A Charter for the Disabled*, Oxford, Blackwell.

Townsend, P. (1979) *Poverty in the United Kingdom*, Harmondsworth, Penguin.

Trieschmann, R. B. (1980) *Spinal Cord Injuries*, Oxford, Pergamon Press.

Tuckey, R. and Tuckey L. (1981) *An Ordinary Place*, Windsor, NFER—Nelson.

UPIAS (1976) *Fundamental Principles of Disability*, London, Union of Physically Impaired Against Segregation.

Walker, A. and Townsend, P. (eds) (1981) *Disability in Britain*, London, Martin Robertson.

Warnock Report (1978) *Special Educational Needs: Report of the Committee of Enquiry into the Education of Children and Young People*, London, HMSO.

Warren, M. D., Knight, R. and Warren, J. L. (1979) *Changing Capabilities and Needs of People with Handicaps*, Health Services Research Unit, University of Kent.

Weller, D. J. and Miller, P. M. (1977) 'Emotional reactions of patient, family, and staff in acute care period of spinal cord injury: part 2', *Social Work in Health Care*, vol. 3.

Wilding, P. (1982) *Professional Power and Social Welfare*, London, Routledge & Kegan Paul.

Wilkin, D. (1979) *Caring for the Mentally Handicapped Child*, London, Croom Helm.

Wolfensberger, W. and Glenn, L. (1975) *Program Analysis of Service Systems (PASS): A Method for the Quantitative Evaluation of Human Services*, 2nd edn, vol. I Handbook; vol. II Field Manual, Toronto, National Institute on Mental Retardation.

World Health Organisation (1980) *International Classification of Impairments, Disabilities and Handicaps*, Geneva, WHO.

Young, M. and Willmott, P. (1973) *The Symmetrical Family*, Harmondsworth, Penguin.

Index